STECK-VAUGHN
CRITICAL THI[NKING]

Reading, Thinking, and Reasoning Skills

Teacher's Edition

Authors

Don Barnes
Professor of Education
Ball State University; Muncie, Indiana

Arlene Burgdorf
Former Resource Consultant
Hammond Indiana Public Schools

L. Stanley Wenck
Professor of Educational Psychology
Ball State University; Muncie, Indiana

Consultant

Gloria Sesso
Supervisor of Social Studies
Half Hollow Hills School District; Dix Hills, New York

LEVEL					
A	B	C	D	E	F

STECK-VAUGHN
C O M P A N Y
A Subsidiary of National Education Corporation

TABLE OF CONTENTS

Contributing Writer: Dr. Martha L. Kendrick, Ed.D.
Instructor of Primary Education
Burris Laboratory School
Ball State University

ISBN 0–8114–6607–8

Teach critical thinking skills in 5 simple steps!

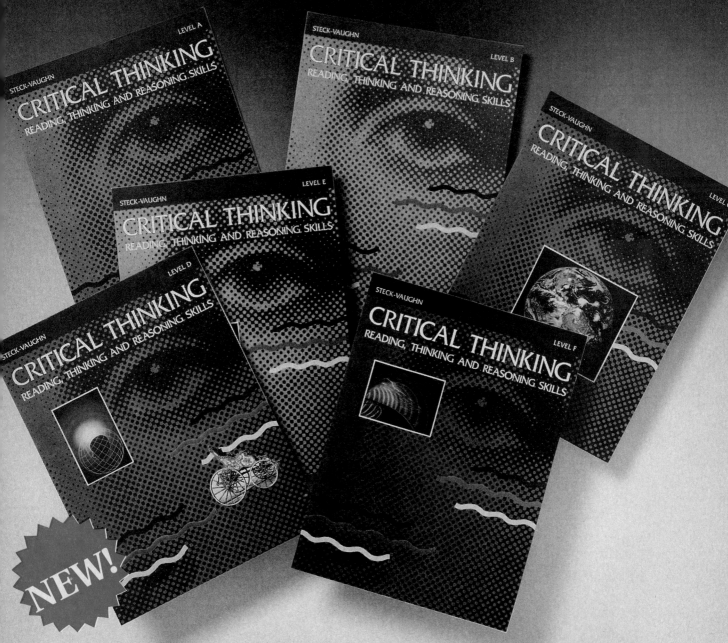

Steck-Vaughn Critical Thinking

CRITICAL THINKING
Up-to-date, exciting, and effective

- **Each unit focuses on one stage of *Bloom's Taxonomy!*** Each book addresses knowing, under-standing, applying, analyzing, synthesizing, and evaluating. (Levels 1 and 2 focus on only the first four stages.)

- **Inviting new unit openers!** Arouse curiosity and lead students into units with a good attitude for learning.

- **Lessons address one skill at a time!** Students master each skill before they move on to the next.

- **"Extending Your Skills" section at the end of each unit!** Brief, two-page reviews provide a convenient mastery check.

- **Six-book sequential program!** Students' critical thinking skills improve as their reading level increases.

- **At-home blackline master for each unit!** Involves parents in reinforcing new knowledge.

- **Exciting presentation!** Students are motivated by the variety of new and challenging activities and current, level-appropriate illustrations.

▶ The activities in *Critical Thinking* are consistent and inviting to students.

UNIT **3**

Applying

Applying means using what you kn...

UNIT **1**

KNOWLEDGE | COMPREHENSION | A

BLOO

UNIT 1: KNOWING

Skill 1	Classifying	PAGES
Skill 2	Real and Fanciful	6–10
Skill 3	Fact and Opinion	11–12
Skill 4	Definition and Example	13–16
Skill 5	Outlining and Summarizing	17–20
		21–24

...picture. How does ...her arms raised? ...pecial day? What ...o to win the ...felt the way ...ny?

T-10

SKILL 31 ⟨ Developing Criteria ⟩

A. Imagine that you are buying books for each of the people described below. Use what you read about each person to choose the books they would enjoy most. Write the letters of the best book choices before each name.

 a. Jellybean—The Talking Mouse Supreme
b. FUN WITH SCIENCE
 c. FACTS ABOUT FISH
d. FAMOUS INVENTORS

e. THE PET STORE MYSTERY
f. MONSTER TALES
g. All About Magnets

1. _____ Alex—He is interested in animals. He enjoys working at his mom's pet store. He has a big aquarium at home. He likes to read about real and imaginary animals.

2. _____ Sara—She loves science. She likes to build things, try to figure out how things work, and solve all kinds of mysteries. She would like to be an inventor when she grows up.

B. What things do you keep in mind when you choose a book for yourself? _____

_____

Decide which book shown above you might enjoy. Write its title and give two reasons for your choice.

_____

_____

 Critical Thinking, Level C © 1993 Steck-Vaughn

Name _____

114

Classifying

SKILL 1 PAGES 6–10

STEP ONE Define the Skill

Discuss with your pupils the meaning of *classifying*: grouping things, people, or ideas because they are alike in some way.

STEP TWO Identify the Steps

Explain to your students the steps they need to follow to classify any group of items, large or small:
1. Look at the items and decide which are alike in some way.
2. Place the like things together in one group.
3. Give a name to each group.
4. See if you can classify the items in one group into smaller groups.

STEP THREE Demonstrate the Skill

Ask pupils to watch and listen as you classify a group of items, following Step Two. SUGGESTION: On the board, write the names of different animals in random order. Then write three numbered categories—*pets, farm animals, wild animals*. Number animals by category, explaining why you are grouping them this way. Show pupils that one category may also be divided into smaller categories—for example, poodles and beagles are kinds of pet dogs; pet dogs, along with some pets, farm animals, and wild animals are furry animals.

STEP FOUR Practice the Skill

Use pages 6–10. See *Teacher Note* on each page.

STEP FIVE Provide Feedback

Discuss pupils' answers. METACOGNITION: Ask pupils to describe what they did. You may need to ask: How did you decide whether certain things were alike? What did you look at or think about? How did you decide what name to give each group?

ENRICHMENT ACTIVITIES

Present several categories, such as things that have wheels and things that grow. Challenge groups of pupils to list as many things for each category as they can in a certain amount of time.

Have pupils build a word web indicating how an item such as scissors may be used. Angled out from the word *scissors* might be *haircut, surgery, sewing, and cut paper.*

Classify animals according to where they might live. Help pupils conclude that some animals may live in several different areas. A horse might be at a circus, on a farm, or in the wild; a snake might be on a farm and in a jungle.

Real and Fanciful

SKILL 2 PAGES 11–12

STEP ONE Define the Skill

Discuss with your pupils the meaning of knowing the difference between *real and fanciful*: knowing the difference between things that are real and things that are only imagined.

STEP TWO Identify the Steps

Explain to your pupils the steps they need to follow to tell the difference between real and fanciful:
1. Look at a picture carefully or read the words carefully.
2. Decide whether the picture or the words tell about something that can really happen or something that can only be imagined.

STEP THREE Demonstrate the Skill

Ask pupils to watch and listen as you show the difference between real and fanciful, following Step Two. SUGGESTION: Write two sample sentences on the board—*My family lives in a brown brick house* and *My family lives in a magician's mirror.* Point out that the sentences are the same except for the final phrases. The last phrase in the first sentence describes a place where a family really could live; the last phrase in the second sentence does not. Therefore, the first statement could be real; the second is imaginary, or fanciful.

STEP FOUR Practice the Skill

Use pages 11–12. See *Teacher Note* on each page.

STEP FIVE Provide Feedback

Discuss pupils' answers. METACOGNITION: Ask pupils to describe what they did. You may need to ask: How did you decide which things were real and which were fanciful? How did you decide which statements were real and which were fanciful?

Unit 1 **T-11**

Knowing

TAXONOMY

| ...YSIS | SYNTHESIS | EVALUATION |

...is the term used in Bloom's ...he first stage in cognitive ...is starting point includes both ...f information and the ability ...mation when needed.

...s program have identified the ...being particularly helpful in ...'s first stage:

...Between Real and Fanciful
...Between Fact and Opinion
...Between Definition and ...

...res for teaching each of these ...son plans will help you use ...as you incorporate *thinking* ...ng day. Enrichment activities ...sson will help your students ...red thinking skills to a ...

...completed, copy and ...ne Newsletter on

School-Home Newsletters for each unit include motivating At-Home activities that reinforce skills.

New and expanded teacher editions include a comprehensive introduction to each unit. Lesson pages are level appropriate and include stimulating enrichment activities to challenge students in different ways.

Thinker's Corner

SCHOOL-HOME NEWSLETTER

UNIT 4
ANALYZING

In the fourth unit of *Critical Thinking: Reading, Thinking, and Reasoning Skills,* your child has been studying the following skills:

- judging completeness
- relevance of information
- abstract or concrete
- logic of actions
- elements of a selection
- story logic
- recognizing fallacies

This newsletter is designed to provide an important link between home and school. You can support your child's learning habits by asking what he or she has learned in school and by discussing papers brought home. You may also wish to do some of the activities suggested in this newsletter.

What's Missing?

Have your child work with judging completeness by asking him or her to trace a picture of an object but to leave something out, such as a wagon without a wheel. Then your child should ask other family members if they can find out what's missing.

Can You Draw an Idea?

Help your child distinguish between concrete and abstract things by asking him or her to draw a picture of each of the following: *dog, love, chicken, shoe, idea,*

dream. Ask which are concrete things and which are abstract things. It will probably be much easier to draw a picture of the concrete things, because they can be seen, heard, felt, smelled, and tasted. Abstract things, such as *love, idea,* and *dream,* are not easy to picture.

Does This Make Sense?

Have fun with discussing logic of actions by asking your child to think of silly things to do, such as taking a bath on Main Street or swimming in syrup. After each suggestion, ask your child why each statement may not make sense.

Who, What, When, Where, How?

You can help your child understand the elements of a story by talking about a book he or she has recently read. Example questions are:

- Who are the main characters in the story?
- What happened in the story?
- When and where did the story take place?
- How did the story end?

Commercial Alert

You can help your child recognize fallacies in commercials. The next time you see or hear a commercial that makes certain claims, discuss with your child what the commercial is trying to convince you of. For example, will eating a certain cereal or wearing a certain shoe make you as good as a certain sports star?

Teach critical thinking skills in 5 simple steps

This is an all-new edition of *Steck-Vaughn Critical Thinking,* but one thing hasn't changed: the acclaimed 5-step lesson plan. This thorough, predictable instructional approach has helped thousands of students develop reading and reasoning skills that will serve them for a lifetime.

1 Define the Skill
Discuss the meaning of classifying with your pupils: grouping ideas, objects, or people according to things they have in common.

2 Identify the Steps
Explain to your pupils the steps they need to follow to classify any group of items, large or small.

3 Demonstrate the Skill
Ask pupils to watch and listen as you classify a group of items, following the four steps.

4 Practice the Skill
Use pages 6-10 to give pupils an opportunity to practice classifying

5 Provide Feedback
Have pupils correct and discuss their answers.

The 5-step lesson plan is back!

Bigger, better Teacher's Editions

- **At-home; enrichment activities!** Sixteen new pages per book include parent-involvement activities and three types of all-new enrichment activities.

- **Level-appropriate Teacher's Edition introductions!** Teachers can model lessons on an appropriate example at each level.

- **Comprehensive lesson plans!** Clarify instructional theories, goals, and mechanics.

- **Lessons written in conversational tone include examples which demonstrate each skill!** Teachers can present lessons right out of the book with minimal preparation.

- **Scope and Sequence charts!** Correlate skills to appropriate page numbers in each book.

- **Progress chart blackline master!** Allows teachers to record and monitor each pupil's achievements.

SCOPE & SEQUENCE

	Level A	Level B	Level C	Level D	Level E	Level F
UNIT 1 Knowing	**5**	**5**	**5**	**5**	**5**	**5**
Skill 1 Classifying	6–10	6–10	6–10	6–10	6–8	6–8
Skill 2 Real and Make-Believe	11–14	11–14	11–12	11–12	9–10	9–10
Skill 3 Fact and Opinion	15–18	15–18	13–16	13–16	11–12	11–14
Skill 4 Definition and Example	19–22	19–22	17–20	17–20	13–14	15–16
Skill 5 Outlining and Summarizing	23–26	23–26	21–24	21–24	15–18	17–20
UNIT 2 Understanding	**29**	**29**	**27**	**27**	**21**	**23**
Skill 6 Comparing and Contrasting	30–32	30–32	28–30	28–30	22–24	24–26
Skill 7 Identifying Structure	33–34	33–34	31–32	31–32	25–26	27–28
Skill 8 Steps in a Process	35–38	35–38	33–34	33–34	27–28	29–30
Skill 9 Understanding Pictures	39–40	39–40	35–36	35–36	29–30	31–32
Skill 10 Comparing Word Meanings	41–42	41–42	37–38	37–38	31–32	33–34
Skill 11 Identifying Main Ideas	43–46	43–46	39–42	39–42	33–34	35–36
Skill 12 Identifying Relationships	47–50	47–50	43–46	43–46	35–38	37–40
UNIT 3 Applying	**53**	**53**	**49**	**49**	**41**	**43**
Skill 13 Ordering Objects	54–56	54–56	50–52	50–52	42–44	44–46
Skill 14 Estimating	57–60	57–60	53–54	53–54	45–46	47–48
Skill 15 Thinking About What Will Happen	61–64	61–64	55–58	55–58	47–48	49–50
Skill 16 Inferring	65–68	65–68	59–62	59–62	49–52	51–54
Skill 17 Changes in Word Meanings	69–70	69–72	63–66	63–64	53–56	55–56

	Level A	Level B	Level C	Level D	Level E	Level F
UNIT 4 Analyzing	**73**	**75**	**69**	**67**	**59**	**59**
Skill 18 Judging Completeness	74–76	76–78	70–72	68–70	60–62	60–62
Skill 19 Thinking About Facts That Fit	77–80	79–80	73–74	71–72	63–64	63–64
Skill 20 Abstract or Concrete	81–84	81–84	75–76	73–74	65–66	65–66
Skill 21 Logic of Actions	85–88	85–88	77–78	75–76	67–68	67–68
Skill 22 Parts of a Story	89–90	89–90	79–80	77–78	69–70	69–70
Skill 23 Story Logic	91–94	91–92	81–82	79–80	71–72	71–72
Skill 24 Recognizing True and False		93–94	83–86	81–84	73–76	73–76
UNIT 5 Synthesizing			**89**	**87**	**79**	**79**
Skill 25 Communicating Ideas			90–92	88–90	80–82	80–82
Skill 26 Planning Projects			93–94	91–94	83–86	83–86
Skill 27 Building Hypotheses			95–98	95–98	87–90	87–90
Skill 28 Drawing Conclusions			99–102	99–102	91–96	91–96
Skill 29 Proposing Alternatives			103–106	103–106	97–102	97–102
UNIT 6 Evaluating			**109**	**109**	**105**	**105**
Skill 30 Testing Generalizations			110–112	110–112	106–108	106–108
Skill 31 Developing Criteria			113–114	113–114	109–112	109–112
Skill 32 Judging Accuracy			115–118	115–118	113–116	113–116
Skill 33 Making Decisions			119–122	119–122	117–120	117–120
Skill 34 Identifying Values			123–124	123–124	121–124	121–124
Skill 35 Mood of a Story			125–126	125–126	125–126	125–126

CORRELATION TO CONTENT AREAS

	Level A	Level B	Level C	Level D	Level E	Level F
Reading and Language Arts	12, 13, 14, 15, 16, 17, 18, 22, 23, 26, 30, 34, 35, 36, 37, 41, 42, 43, 44, 45, 46, 51, 52, 55, 65, 66, 67, 68, 69, 70, 71, 72, 75, 79, 80, 83, 84, 88, 89, 90, 91, 92, 93, 94, 95, 96	7, 9, 11, 12, 13, 14, 15, 16, 17, 20, 21, 22, 24, 25, 27, 28, 32, 34, 35, 37, 41, 42, 43, 45, 46, 50, 52, 61, 62, 63, 65, 67, 68, 69, 70, 71, 72, 74, 78, 80, 82, 88, 89, 90, 91, 92, 94, 96	6, 11, 12, 13, 14, 15, 16, 25, 29, 30, 31, 32, 37, 38, 39, 40, 43, 44, 45, 46, 48, 55, 56, 57, 59, 60, 61, 62, 63, 64, 65, 66, 67, 68, 70, 72, 73, 74, 75, 77, 78, 79, 80, 81, 82, 83, 84, 85, 86, 87, 88, 93, 95, 96, 97, 98, 101, 102, 110, 112, 116, 117, 119, 120, 121, 122, 123, 124, 125, 126, 128	7, 11, 12, 13, 14, 15, 16, 19, 20, 21, 26, 30, 31, 32, 33, 36, 37, 38, 39, 40, 42, 44, 45, 48, 55, 56, 57, 58, 59, 61, 62, 63, 64, 65, 66, 67, 69, 70, 71, 73, 75, 76, 77, 78, 79, 80, 81, 82, 83, 84, 85, 88, 89, 95, 96, 97, 98, 99, 100, 104, 105, 106, 112, 113, 116, 117, 119, 120, 121, 123, 124, 125, 126, 128	9, 10, 11, 12, 13, 15, 16, 19, 23, 24, 25, 26, 27, 31, 32, 35, 37, 39, 42, 47, 48, 49, 50, 51, 52, 53, 54, 55, 56, 57, 58, 61, 65, 66, 67, 69, 70, 71, 73, 74, 75, 76, 77, 78, 80, 82, 83, 87, 88, 89, 90, 92, 93, 94, 97, 98, 99, 100, 102, 106, 107, 111, 112, 117, 120, 121, 122, 123, 125, 126, 128	6, 9, 11, 15, 16, 17, 18, 19, 20, 22, 25, 26, 27, 33, 34, 35, 36, 38, 39, 40, 42, 51, 52, 53, 55, 56, 58, 60, 62, 64, 66, 68, 70, 71, 73, 76, 78, 82, 88, 89, 95, 96, 102, 113, 115, 120, 123, 125, 126, 128
Social Studies	7, 8, 9, 10, 20, 25, 49, 54, 61, 76, 77, 78, 85, 87	6, 8, 10, 18, 23, 26, 31, 33, 38, 47, 48, 49, 64, 66, 77, 79, 81, 85, 86, 87, 90	7, 9, 10, 22, 23, 26, 28, 33, 35, 42, 47, 76, 90, 92, 100, 103, 104, 105, 106, 107, 108, 114, 115, 118, 127	6, 8, 9, 10, 24, 25, 28, 46, 50, 58, 72, 74, 86, 91, 92, 93, 101, 103, 115, 118, 122	7, 14, 15, 17, 28, 33, 36, 38, 44, 57, 60, 62, 63, 64, 68, 70, 81, 84, 85, 101, 113, 114, 116, 118, 119, 127	7, 12, 13, 14, 29, 30, 32, 35, 37, 41, 45, 50, 54, 57, 63, 65, 67, 69, 72, 74, 75, 83, 85, 90, 92, 97, 98, 99, 100, 101, 102, 108, 110, 112, 113, 114, 117, 118, 119, 121, 122, 123, 124
Science	6, 11, 19, 21, 24, 27, 28, 36, 38, 47, 48, 50, 62, 63, 64, 81, 86	19, 25, 44, 51, 64, 80, 93, 95	17, 18, 19, 20, 21, 23, 24, 34, 39, 41, 58, 90, 94, 99, 111, 113	17, 18, 22, 23, 29, 41, 43, 52, 90, 94, 107, 108, 110, 111, 114	6, 8, 18, 20, 22, 33, 34, 40, 72, 86, 91, 96, 103, 104, 108, 110, 115, 124	8, 10, 19, 24, 45, 46, 49, 61, 77, 80, 81, 84, 86, 87, 91, 93, 94, 98, 103, 106, 107, 116
Math	31, 32, 33, 39, 40, 54, 56, 57, 58, 59, 60, 74, 82	30, 36, 39, 40, 54, 55, 56, 57, 58, 59, 60, 73, 76, 83, 84	8, 36, 50, 51, 52, 53, 54, 71, 90, 91, 107	34, 35, 46, 47, 51, 53, 54, 60, 68, 90, 102, 109, 127	29, 30, 42, 43, 45, 46, 95, 109	21, 28, 31, 32, 44, 47, 48, 80, 94, 104, 109, 111, 120, 127

USING THE PROGRAM

Overview

Steck-Vaughn Critical Thinking is a six-book program designed to teach thinking skills. The skills are organized according to Benjamin Bloom's *Taxonomy of Educational Objectives.** At all six levels of the program, pupils are taught skills that have been identified as being particularly helpful in developing Bloom's first four stages of thinking—Knowledge, Comprehension, Application, and Analysis. At Levels C–F, pupils move into the higher-level skills of Synthesis and Evaluation.

Program Philosophy

Direct teaching of thinking skills provides pupils with the opportunity to focus on *thinking* rather than on specific content. Once pupils have begun to consider themselves "thinkers," they will be better able to learn and make use of content area material. *Steck-Vaughn Critical Thinking* is designed to help teach your pupils to think. This Teacher's Edition includes step-by-step lesson plans for teaching each of the twenty-four thinking skills which are found on pages T-10 through T-29 in this level.

Pupils need to practice newly acquired skills in order to retain them. Pupils who have had the opportunity to practice skills are better able to transfer them to other areas of the curriculum. *Steck-Vaughn Critical Thinking* contains practice pages for every skill presented in the program, as well as suggestions for enrichment activities.

Pupils need to know whether or not they are on the right track when they are practicing a new skill. Without feedback, a pupil might continue to practice a skill incorrectly. *Steck-Vaughn Critical Thinking* encourages the use of feedback. In addition, the program ties *metacognitive skills* to each lesson. Each lesson plan suggests questions to make your pupils "think about their thinking," as you discuss their responses to items on the practice pages.

Implementing the Program

The Scope and Sequence Chart on pages T-6 and T-7 of this guide identifies the skills taught in each level of *Steck-Vaughn Critical Thinking.* A complete lesson plan is provided for teaching each of these skills. Every lesson plan presents a five-step procedure that will help you use the program more easily:

STEP ONE: Define the Skill
In this step, you are given a definition that will help you explain the skill to your pupils.

STEP TWO: Identify the Steps
Here you are provided with concrete steps that your pupils can use as they learn the skill.

STEP THREE: Demonstrate the Skill
A suggestion is provided for demonstrating the skill to your pupils.

STEP FOUR: Practice the Skill
The pages developed for practicing the skill are listed for your convenience. In addition, each page in the text includes a *Teacher Note* that provides specific suggestions for using that page.

STEP FIVE: Provide Feedback
Questions are provided to help you get your pupils to "think about their thinking" (metacognition).

Each lesson plan also includes three suggestions for engaging pupils in meaningful enrichment activities. When your pupils can apply a new skill to material learned previously, they are demonstrating that they have truly mastered the new skill.

Involving the home in children's educational growth is of key importance. To encourage this involvement, School-Home Newsletters highlight the skills in the units and include activities that parents or guardians can do to reinforce the skills with their children.

The Class Assessment Summary is included for ease in tracking skill mastery by individual class members.

* Bloom, Benjamin. *Taxonomy of Educational Objectives, Handbook 1: Cognitive Domain.* New York: David McKay Company, Inc. 1956

UNIT
1

Knowing

BLOOM'S TAXONOMY

| KNOWLEDGE | COMPREHENSION | APPLICATION | ANALYSIS | SYNTHESIS | EVALUATION |

UNIT I: KNOWING	PAGES
Skill 1 Classifying	6 – 10
Skill 2 Real and Make-Believe	11 – 14
Skill 3 Fact and Opinion	15 – 18
Skill 4 Definition and Example	19 – 22
Skill 5 Outlining and Summarizing	23 – 26

KNOWLEDGE is the term used in Bloom's Taxonomy for the first stage in cognitive development. This starting point includes both the acquisition of information and the ability to recall the information when needed.

The authors of this program have identified the following skills as being particularly helpful in developing Bloom's first stage:

1. Classifying
2. Discriminating Between Real and Make-Believe
3. Discriminating Between Fact and Opinion
4. Discriminating Between Definition and Example
5. Outlining and Summarizing

Step-by-step procedures for teaching each of these skills follow. These lesson plans will help you use the program with ease as you incorporate *thinking skills* into your teaching day. Enrichment activities that accompany each lesson will help your students apply their newly acquired thinking skills to a variety of situations.

After this unit has been completed, copy and distribute the School-Home Newsletter on pages T-32 and T-33.

Classifying

STEP ONE Define the Skill

Discuss with your pupils the meaning of *classifying:* **putting things, people, or ideas together because they are alike in some way.**

STEP TWO Identify the Steps

Explain to your pupils the steps they need to follow to classify any group of items, large or small:
1. Look at the items and decide which are alike in some way.
2. Place the like things together in one group.
3. Give a name to each group.

STEP THREE Demonstrate the Skill

Ask pupils to watch and listen as you classify a group of items, following Step Two.

SUGGESTION: Write the names of these animals on the board—*whale, elephant, cow, robin, fish, bluejay, rat.* Then write three numbered categories—*animals that live on land, animals that live in water, animals that fly.* Write the name of each animal under the appropriate category, explaining why you are grouping them in this way.

STEP FOUR Practice the Skill

Use pages 6–10. See *Teacher Note* on each page.

STEP FIVE Provide Feedback

Discuss pupils' answers. **METACOGNITION:** Ask pupils to describe what they did. You may need to ask: **How did you decide which things belonged together?**

ENRICHMENT ACTIVITIES

Challenge pupils to name a friend, a food, and an article of clothing that have names beginning with the same initial consonant.

Name three items and challenge pupils to explain what they have in common and how one is different. For example: *a bird, cat, and dog are all animals, each may be a pet, but a bird is the only one that flies.*

Fill a table with items that have been "borrowed" from locations such as the gym, art room, and music room. Let pupils select an item to return to its proper room. Take a class tour and deliver the items to each teacher who needs them. You may then wish to ask pupils to each bring one item from home. Have volunteers classify the items to an appropriate room.

Real and Make-Believe

STEP ONE Define the Skill

Discuss with your pupils the meaning of telling the difference between *real and make-believe* things: **telling the difference between things that can actually be and things that are only imagined.**

STEP TWO Identify the Steps

Explain to your pupils the steps they need to follow to tell the difference between real and make-believe things:
1. Look at a picture carefully or read the words carefully.
2. Decide whether the picture or words tell about something that could really happen or something that happens only in your imagination.

STEP THREE Demonstrate the Skill

Ask pupils to watch and listen as you tell the difference between real and make-believe, following

Step Two. **SUGGESTION:** Write two sentences on the board—for example, *Jake's pet frog croaked,* and *Jake's pet frog said hello.* Read the sentences aloud and point out that they are the same except for the frog's action. Explain that the action described in the first sentence describes something that could happen in real life, while the action in the second is make-believe.

STEP FOUR Practice the Skill

Use pages 11–14. See *Teacher Note* on each page.

STEP FIVE Provide Feedback

Discuss pupils' answers. **METACOGNITION:** Ask pupils to describe what they did. You may need to ask: **How did you decide which sentences told about something make-believe and which told about something real?**

As a group, write a realistic story about a boy and his dog. Then write a make-believe version of the same story. Discuss how stories change when make-believe elements are added. For example, the dog may be able to talk to the boy.

Discuss with pupils things they might see or do in an imaginary world. Allow them to depict their imaginary world by making a class mural.

Use some story starters similar to the following to encourage fanciful thinking: *You wake up one morning and find you are only six inches tall.*

SKILL 3   PAGES 15–18   Fact and Opinion

STEP ONE Define the Skill

Discuss with your pupils the meaning of telling the difference between *fact and opinion:* **deciding which sentences can be proved true and which sentences cannot be proved true.**

STEP TWO Identify the Steps

Explain to your pupils the steps they need to follow to tell the difference between fact and opinion:
1. Read a sentence and decide how it could be proved true. If it can be proved true, it's a fact.
2. Look for words such as *think, nice, best,* and *good* in a sentence. They are clues that the sentence tells an opinion.

STEP THREE Demonstrate the Skill

Ask pupils to watch and listen as you tell the difference between fact and opinion, following Step Two. **SUGGESTION:** Write two sentences on the

board—*This song is new,* and *This song is good.* Explain how the first sentence can be proved true (by calling a radio station, checking in a library book, or even asking the person who wrote it). Explain how the second sentence cannot be proved true—some people might think the song is bad. Also, the second sentence has a clue word that it is an opinion *(good)*. However, caution pupils that opinions do not always have clue words.

STEP FOUR Practice the Skill

Use pages 15–18. See *Teacher Note* on each page.

STEP FIVE Provide Feedback

Discuss pupils' answers. **METACOGNITION:** Ask pupils to describe what they did. You may need to ask: **How did you decide which sentences gave facts? How did you decide which sentences gave opinions?**

Read one of *The Magic School Bus* stories by Joanna Cole. Have pupils determine which parts of the story are fact, which parts might be fact, and which parts are not fact.

Take a tour of the classroom, hallway, or school grounds. Point to items or objects and ask pupils for one statement each of fact or opinion. For example: *The picture was drawn by Mandy* (fact). *Mandy is a good artist* (opinion).

Choose a child to role-play a doctor who shows a happy face when patients give specific facts and a sad face for general statements. For example: *My temperature is 102°* (specific). *My arm hurts* (general).

SKILL 4   PAGES 19–22   Definition and Example

STEP ONE Define the Skill

Discuss with your pupils the difference between *definition and example:* **the difference between telling what a word means and naming members of a group the word describes.**

STEP TWO Identify the Steps

Explain the steps pupils need to follow to tell the difference between definitions and examples:
1. Ask yourself, does this sentence tell the meaning of a word? If so, it is a definition.
2. Ask yourself, does this word name a thing that belongs to a group? If so, it is an example.

STEP THREE Demonstrate the Skill

Ask pupils to watch and listen as you tell the difference between a definition of a word and examples of the word, following Step Two.
SUGGESTION: Write this definition on the board—*A fruit is part of a plant. You can eat a fruit.* Then write the names of fruits—*apple, banana, strawberry*—and draw or show pictures as well, if possible. Point out that the sentences tell what a fruit is. They give the definition of a fruit. Then point out how each word and picture fits the definition. Each is a kind of, or an example of, a fruit.

STEP FOUR Practice the Skill

Use pages 19–22. See *Teacher Note* on each page.

STEP FIVE Provide Feedback

Discuss pupils' answers. **METACOGNITION:** Ask pupils to describe what they did. You may need to ask: **How did you match the words with their definitions? How did you match the pictures with the definitions?**

ENRICHMENT ACTIVITIES

Have pupils guess the answers to riddles. For example: *I am made of wax. If you light me, I will burn. What am I?* (candle); *You drink from me. I do not have a handle. What am I?* (glass) Challenge pupils to make up their own riddles.

Display items such as a ball, a block, and a puzzle piece. Have pupils introduce each item by describing its shape, what it is made of, and what it is used for.

Play "Food Inspectors." One pupil draws the name of a food from a container and keeps the name a secret. "Inspectors" ask the pupil questions about the food. The one who guesses the food then becomes the next "Inspector."

SKILL 5 PAGES 23–26   (Outlining and Summarizing)

STEP ONE Define the Skill

Discuss with your pupils the meaning of *outlining and summarizing:* **short ways of presenting information. When we summarize, we only give the main points. When we outline, we give the main point and details in a special form.**

STEP TWO Identify the Steps

Explain to your pupils the steps they need to follow to get ready to summarize and outline:
  1. Think about the main idea—what all the sentences are telling about.
  2. Think how each sentence fits with a main idea. Put it with that idea.

STEP THREE Demonstrate the Skill

Ask pupils to watch and listen as you get ready to summarize and outline, following Step Two.

SUGGESTION: Select a simple story with which your pupils are familiar—for example, *The Three Billy Goats Gruff.* Use words and, if possible, pictures to show how to outline and summarize the story. Identify the "big" ideas—the Troll wants to eat the three Billy Goats Gruff, but they trick the Troll. Identify the "small" ideas that support each big idea—the Troll threatens each goat; the goats cross one at a time; they cross the bridge safely.

STEP FOUR Practice the Skill

Use pages 23–26. See *Teacher Note* on each page.

STEP FIVE Provide Feedback

Discuss pupils' answers. **METACOGNITION:** Ask pupils to describe what they did. You may need to ask: **How did you decide which words were the most important words from the story?**

ENRICHMENT ACTIVITIES

Pupils may enjoy writing stories, exchanging them with classmates, and finding the main ideas and details in each.

Make a class "How To" book. Have each pupil select a relatively simple process that can be described with these steps: *first, next,* and *last.* Pupils may write out the process to be included in the class book.

Go on a "Buildings, Roofs, and Fences" walk. Have groups note building materials (brick, stone, wood); roof lines (flat, sloped, peaked); and fences (wire, chain, wood, metal). Outline the information and have pupils write an informational article.

UNIT 2

Understanding

BLOOM'S TAXONOMY

KNOWLEDGE	COMPREHENSION	APPLICATION	ANALYSIS	SYNTHESIS	EVALUATION

COMPREHENSION is the term used in Bloom's Taxonomy for the second stage in cognitive development. Comprehension refers to the basic level of understanding and involves the ability to know what is being communicated in order to make use of the information. This includes translating or interpreting a communication or extrapolating information from a communication.

The authors of this program have identified the following skills as being particularly helpful in developing Bloom's second stage:

1. Comparing and Contrasting
2. Identifying Structure
3. Identifying Steps in a Process
4. Understanding Pictures
5. Comparing Word Meanings
6. Identifying Main Ideas
7. Identifying Relationships

Step-by-step procedures for teaching each of these skills follow. These lesson plans will help you use the program with ease as you incorporate *thinking skills* into your teaching day. Enrichment activities that accompany each lesson will help your students apply their newly acquired thinking skills to a variety of situations.

After this unit has been completed, copy and distribute the School-Home Newsletter on pages T-34 and T-35.

Comparing and Contrasting

STEP ONE Define the Skill

Discuss with your pupils the meaning of *comparing and contrasting:* **looking at things and deciding how they are alike and how they are different.**

STEP TWO Identify the Steps

Explain to your pupils the steps they need to follow to compare and contrast two or more items:
1. Look carefully to see how the items are alike.
2. Look carefully to see how the items are different.

STEP THREE Demonstrate the Skill

Ask pupils to watch and listen as you compare and contrast items, following Step Two. **SUGGESTION:** Select two storybook characters, for example, Hansel and Gretel, or a boy and a girl from a story in your pupils' reader. Tell how the two are alike—*both have two eyes, a nose, a mouth*, and so on. Then tell how they are different—*one is a girl, the other a boy; one is taller than the other*; and so on.

STEP FOUR Practice the Skill

Use pages 30–32. See *Teacher Note* on each page.

STEP FIVE Provide Feedback

Discuss pupils' answers. **METACOGNITION:** Ask pupils to describe what they did. You may need to ask: **How did you decide which things were different? How did you decide which things were alike? What did you look at to compare things?**

ENRICHMENT ACTIVITIES

Declare a hat day and have pupils parade their hats. Then have pupils choose two hats and explain one way they are alike and one way they are different.

Provide three transparent containers of water. Add a drop of food coloring, a packet of salt, or a spoonful of coffee creamer to each container. Ask pupils to contrast the results.

After reading *The Three Little Pigs*, challenge one group of pupils to think about as many similarities about the pigs as they can. Write these under a category titled *Similar* on the board. Then have another group list as many differences as possible. After you have written these on the board under a *Different* category, encourage pupils to compare and contrast the two groups.

Identifying Structure

STEP ONE Define the Skill

Discuss with your pupils the meaning of *identifying structure:* **looking at the parts of something and seeing how the parts fit together to make the whole thing.**

STEP TWO Identify the Steps

Explain to your pupils the steps they need to follow to identify the structure of something:
1. Look at the whole thing and decide what it is.
2. Look at the parts and list them.
3. See how the parts fit together.
4. See how the parts together make the whole thing.

STEP THREE Demonstrate the Skill

Ask pupils to watch and listen as you identify the structure of something, following Step Two.

SUGGESTION: Write the first stanza of the song "Farmer in the Dell" on the board. List the parts—*lines, words, melody*. The parts are arranged in four lines; the same words appear on lines 1, 2, and 4. Point out how the words, lines, and melody all help make up the whole song.

STEP FOUR Practice the Skill

Use pages 33–34. See *Teacher Note* on each page.

STEP FIVE Provide Feedback

Discuss pupils' answers. **METACOGNITION:** Ask pupils to describe what they did. You may need to ask: **How did you identify the special parts of each thing? How did you figure out which letter to change to make a new word?**

ENRICHMENT ACTIVITIES

To show the structure of a family, have pupils create a family tree that includes a father, mother, brothers, and sisters.

Have pupils compare the structures of a birdhouse and a doghouse; a barn and a silo; and a house and an apartment building.

Have each pupil draw a person's head, face, and neck on the top third of a piece of paper. Pupils then exchange papers and draw a torso on the middle third. They exchange again and draw legs and feet. Use the drawings to discuss body parts.

SKILL 8 PAGES 35–38

Steps in a Process

STEP ONE Define the Skill
Discuss with your pupils the meaning of identifying *steps in a process:* **seeing how certain things are done in a step-by-step way and planning the steps you need to take to finish these things.**

STEP TWO Identify the Steps
Explain to your pupils the steps they need to follow to identify steps in a process:
1. What are you trying to do?
2. Decide what is the last thing to happen—the last step.
3. Decide what is the first thing to happen—the first step.
4. Figure out the in-between steps and their order.
5. Check to see whether any steps are missing.

STEP THREE Demonstrate the Skill
Ask pupils to watch and listen as you identify the steps in a process, following Step Two. **SUGGESTION:** List, in random order, the actions needed to give a birthday card—*pick a card, seal the envelope, sign the card, lick the envelope, put the card in the envelope.* Point out that the last step is sealing the envelope. The first is picking the card. Then number the remaining steps in order. Check to see if any steps have been left out.

STEP FOUR Practice the Skill
Use pages 35–38. See *Teacher Note* on each page.

STEP FIVE Provide Feedback
Discuss pupils' answers. **METACOGNITION:** Ask pupils to describe what they did. You may need to ask: **How did you know which steps come first? Which steps come second? Which come last?**

ENRICHMENT ACTIVITIES

Count each school day by putting a straw in a can marked *ones.* When ten straws have accumulated, bundle them with a rubber band and put them in a larger can marked *tens.* Every few days have pupils count the tens and ones and name the number of days that have passed.

Have pairs of pupils sit back-to-back. As one pupil draws a design, he or she tells the other student the kind and direction of marks for the partner to duplicate. When the design is complete, have pupils compare their results.

Have pupils fold a piece of paper to get four boxes. Then have pupils draw four pictures to depict steps in a process related to a daily happening. For example: *getting in a car, brushing teeth,* or *doing schoolwork.*

SKILL 9 PAGES 39–40 — Understanding Pictures

STEP ONE Define the Skill
Discuss with your pupils the meaning of *understanding pictures:* **using pictures to get information and to see connections between things.**

STEP TWO Identify the Steps
Explain to your pupils the steps they need to follow to understand pictures:
1. Look at the whole picture to see what the picture is about.
2. Look at the parts of the picture to see what else you can find out.

STEP THREE Demonstrate the Skill
Ask pupils to watch and listen as you show how you understand a picture, following Step Two. **SUGGESTION:** Draw a very simple map showing your school and its relation to another spot—perhaps a park or the library—two or three blocks away. Explain how the drawing can help you get from one spot to another. Point out that it also shows the streets you would take and the things you would pass on the way.

STEP FOUR Practice the Skill
Use pages 39–40. See *Teacher Note* on each page.

STEP FIVE Provide Feedback
Discuss pupils' answers. **METACOGNITION:** Ask pupils to describe what they did. You may need to ask: **How did you spot the smaller pictures within the bigger picture?**

ENRICHMENT ACTIVITIES

Pupils may enjoy making a chart that identifies the parts of several animals, such as birds, fish, and horses.

Cut in half some scenes from magazines and paste one half on a sheet of paper. Then ask pupils to draw people, animals, and/or objects to complete the other half of the picture.

Have pupils make a map of the setting for a story such as *The Little Red Hen* or *The Three Little Pigs.* Be sure they depict important locations of the story, such as the wheat fields, a path to the mill, or the straw peddler's shop.

SKILL 10 PAGES 41–42 — Comparing Word Meanings

STEP ONE Define the Skill
Discuss with your pupils the meaning of *comparing word meanings:* **seeing how words are alike or different in meaning.**

STEP TWO Identify the Steps
Explain to your pupils the steps they need to follow to compare word meanings:
1. Look at the word and say it.
2. Decide what the word means.
3. Think of words that mean almost the same thing.
4. Think of words that mean the opposite.

STEP THREE Demonstrate the Skill
Ask pupils to watch and listen as you compare word meanings, following Step Two. **SUGGESTION:** Draw or show pictures of two faces—one very happy, the other sad. Write these sentences on the board and read them—*Kelly got a good grade on her report card. She is happy.* Then ask pupils which person could be Kelly. Write *happy* under that picture, then list other words that could also be used—*glad, joyful, cheerful.* Write *sad* under the sad face and list synonyms for it and antonyms for *happy—unhappy, sorrowful, gloomy.*

STEP FOUR Practice the Skill
Use pages 41–42. See *Teacher Note* on each page.

STEP FIVE Provide Feedback
Discuss pupils' answers. **METACOGNITION:** Ask pupils to describe what they did. You may need to ask: **How did you decide which word meant the same as another word? How did you decide which word meant the opposite of another word?**

Begin with a sentence such as *You can throw a rock.* Ask for a synonym for the word *throw.* Use the synonym in the sentence and then ask for other synonyms. Discuss the difference in meaning with each new word.

Play "Who Am I?" Give a riddle about a word that could also be a person's name. Have pupils guess the word. For example: *I'm the kind of class that teaches people how to draw. Who am I?* (Art) Other possible names: *Bill, Pat, Bob, Mark, Penny.*

Read *The King Who Rained* by Fred Gwynne. Start a class collection of idiomatic words and phrases. Make a picture for each one. For example: *goose bumps, don't cut in line, growing like a weed.*

SKILL 11 PAGES 43–46

Identifying Main Ideas

STEP ONE Define the Skill

Discuss with your pupils the meaning of *identifying main ideas:* **seeing the main point in a picture or story.**

STEP TWO Identify the Steps

Explain to your pupils the steps they need to follow to identify main ideas:
1. Look at the picture or read the story.
2. Decide what the picture or story is about.
3. Find the main idea in a sentence or put it in your own words.

STEP THREE Demonstrate the Skill

Ask pupils to watch and listen as you identify the main idea of a paragraph, following Step Two. **SUGGESTION:** Write this story on the board— *Sandy's team won the game in the most exciting way. Sandy hit a home run. She ran around the bases. Everyone on her side cheered. Then they all went home*

happy. Read the paragraph. Note that the way Sandy's team won the game is the main point. Find the sentence with the main idea—the first sentence. Note how the other sentences tell about that point. Erase the first sentence and show how you can also tell the main point just by reading the other sentences.

STEP FOUR Practice the Skill

Use pages 43–46. See *Teacher Note* on each page.

STEP FIVE Provide Feedback

Discuss pupils' answers. **METACOGNITION:** Ask pupils to describe what they did. You may need to ask: **How did you choose the sentence that told the main idea? How did you decide which title best fit each story? How did you choose the sentence that told the main idea of the story?**

Have pupils choose from several titles, such as *A Special Day, My Favorite Hobby,* or *Going on Vacation.* Have them write a story and underline the main idea.

Divide the class into five or six groups. Have each group write a story that is three or four sentences long about a classroom happening. Then on another sheet of paper, have groups write a title for their story. Have a different group match each story with its title.

Pupils may enjoy making a word web related to summer. Then guide pupils as they use the web to decide on a main idea, find details that support the main idea, and write a short story about summer.

Identifying Relationships

STEP ONE   Define the Skill

Discuss with your pupils the meaning of *identifying relationships:* **seeing how two or more things, ideas, or happenings go together in some way.**

STEP TWO   Identify the Steps

Explain to your pupils the steps they need to follow to identify relationships:

1. Read carefully. Think about the things or ideas you are reading about.
2. Ask yourself how these things or ideas go together. What things belong in groups? What ideas belong with each other?

STEP THREE   Demonstrate the Skill

Ask pupils to watch and listen as you identify relationships, following Step Two. **SUGGESTION:** Write the following words on the board—*leaves*, *smile, rain, branches, umbrella, happy*. Read the words and pick out the things that belong together. Explain how the things are related. For example, *leaves and branches* are related because they are parts of trees and bushes, *umbrella* and *rain* are related because an umbrella is used to keep a person dry when it rains, and *smile* and *happy* are related because people often smile when they are happy.

STEP FOUR   Practice the Skill

Use pages 47–50. See *Teacher Note* on each page.

STEP FIVE   Provide Feedback

Discuss pupils' answers. **METACOGNITION:** Ask pupils to describe what they did. You may need to ask: **How did you connect ideas in your mind? How did you decide which picture or word fit into each sentence?**

E N R I C H M E N T   A C T I V I T I E S

Play "You Be the Parent." Ask a question to which the answer is *no*. For example: *May I have a cookie now?* Have the group think of a reason for the *no* answer.

Place a paper plate, some plain paper, and a bowl in a row. One at a time, hold up a paper napkin, a plastic fork, markers, a pencil, a measuring cup, and a package of jello. Ask pupils to explain whether the item goes best with the plate, paper, or bowl.

Investigate imagined classroom accidents. For example: *Joey fell against a table and cut his lip.* Possible causes: *untied shoestring, stepped on a pencil and slipped, tripped over an out-of-place chair, raced to get in line.*

UNIT 3

Applying

BLOOM'S TAXONOMY

KNOWLEDGE	COMPREHENSION	APPLICATION	ANALYSIS	SYNTHESIS	EVALUATION

APPLICATION is the term used in Bloom's Taxonomy for the third stage in cognitive development. Application is the ability to use a learned skill in a new situation.

The authors of this program have identified the following skills as being particularly helpful in developing Bloom's third stage:

1. Ordering Objects
2. Estimating
3. Thinking About What Will Happen
4. Inferring
5. Interpreting Changes in Word Meanings

Step-by-step procedures for teaching each of these skills follow. These lesson plans will help you use the program with ease as you incorporate *thinking skills* into your teaching day. Enrichment activities that accompany each lesson will help your students apply their newly acquired thinking skills to a variety of situations.

After this unit has been completed, copy and distribute the School-Home Newsletter on pages T-36 and T-37.

Ordering Objects

STEP ONE Define the Skill

Discuss with your pupils the meaning of *ordering objects:* **putting items in order to follow a certain pattern.**

STEP TWO Identify the Steps

Explain to your pupils the steps they need to follow to order objects:
1. Look at the objects.
2. Decide what order or pattern the items follow.
3. Decide which object is first and which is last.
4. Put the in-between objects in order.

STEP THREE Demonstrate the Skill

Ask pupils to watch and listen as you order a group of objects, following Step Two. **SUGGESTION:** Fill several cups with different amounts of water. Leave one cup empty and fill another so it is full. Tell pupils that you will order the cups according to how much water they have. Place the empty cup on one end, the full cup at the other and the remaining cups in order from least amount of water to greatest. Allow pupils to see for themselves the pattern that the order creates.

STEP FOUR Practice the Skill

Use pages 54–56. See *Teacher Note* on each page.

STEP FIVE Provide Feedback

Discuss pupils' answers. **METACOGNITION:** Ask pupils to describe what they did. You may need to ask: **How did you decide which item came first or last? Which came next? How did you figure out which item to draw?**

ENRICHMENT ACTIVITIES

Have pupils list ten foods and order them from their most favorite to their least favorite.

Have small groups choose a topic of interest such as birds, dinosaurs, planets, fruits, or wheels. Have the groups draw a series of pictures (or silhouettes) in order to show the size of several members of the topic group.

Have pupils make flip books to show such actions as a flower growing, an airplane taking off, someone blowing up a balloon, building a sand castle, or making a hand-drawn star.

Estimating

STEP ONE Define the Skill

Discuss with your pupils the meaning of *estimating:* **using what you already know to make a good guess.**

STEP TWO Identify the Steps

Explain to your pupils the steps they need to follow to estimate:
1. Picture the size, time, or amount of the thing you are estimating.
2. Look for other facts you may need in order to estimate.
3. Use the picture in your mind and the facts to make a good guess.

STEP THREE Demonstrate the Skill

Ask pupils to watch and listen as you estimate, following Step Two. **SUGGESTION:** Make several different transparencies showing a person's head with three different-sized hats. Show one of the transparencies to your pupils and explain that you will estimate which hat will fit on the head by picturing the size of the hat on top of the head. Then choose. Emphasize the importance of imagining—or visualizing—when estimating. Show pupils another transparency and ask them to close their eyes to visualize which hat will fit.

STEP FOUR Practice the Skill

Use pages 57–60. See *Teacher Note* on each page.

STEP FIVE Provide Feedback

Discuss pupils' answers. **METACOGNITION:** Ask pupils to describe what they did. You may need to ask: **How did you estimate which object fit best? Could you picture what you were estimating? What else did you look at or think about to come up with a good estimate? How did you estimate the time you would spend doing each action?**

ENRICHMENT ACTIVITIES

Display coins of the same size and have pupils estimate and then check how many coins would be needed to cover surfaces such as a playing card, a flash card, and an 8" x 11" piece of paper.

Have pupils use a stopwatch or watch with a second hand to estimate and check the amount of time used for several class activities. For example, *how long will it take to read a story? sharpen a pencil? draw a picture? walk to recess? sing a song?*

Divide pupils into small groups and give each group a different length of string. Name items in the classroom and have groups estimate and then check whether their string is shorter, longer, or equal to the length of these objects.

SKILL 15 PAGES 61–64 Thinking About What Will Happen

STEP ONE Define the Skill
Discuss with your pupils the meaning of *thinking about what will happen:* **making a good guess about what will happen next.**

STEP TWO Identify the Steps
Explain to your pupils the steps they need to follow when they think about what will happen:
1. Think about the facts you know.
2. Think of things that might happen.
3. Guess which thing is most likely to happen.

STEP THREE Demonstrate the Skill
Ask pupils to watch and listen as you think about what will happen, following Step Two.

SUGGESTION: Describe a situation—*for example, you drop a piece of meat on the kitchen floor, and your pet dog sees it.* Think of things that might happen. Predict which would most likely happen—*the dog will come and quickly eat the meat.*

STEP FOUR Practice the Skill
Use pages 61–64. See *Teacher Note* on each page.

STEP FIVE Provide Feedback
Discuss pupils' answers. **METACOGNITION:** Ask pupils to describe what they did. You may need to ask: **How did you decide what you thought would happen? Did you think of other things that might happen?**

ENRICHMENT ACTIVITIES

Tell pupils the titles of several books. Ask them to use the titles to predict what the books might be about.

Write or draw three things a person might do with a tennis ball. Then have pupils decide which use is the most probable.

Staple a cartoon strip, minus the last frame, to a plain sheet of paper for pupils to see. Ask pupils to provide appropriate words and pictures for the last frame.

SKILL 16 PAGES 65–68 Inferring

STEP ONE Define the Skill
Discuss with your pupils the meaning of *inferring:* **using information that you have to come up with other information.**

STEP TWO Identify the Steps
Explain to your pupils the steps they need to follow to infer:
1. Note carefully the information you are given.
2. Think of what else must be true using that information.

STEP THREE Demonstrate the Skill

Ask pupils to watch and listen as you infer, following Step Two. **SUGGESTION:** Describe a situation to your pupils—for example, *You're sitting in your living room. You hear a crash and glass breaking from the kitchen. Then you hear someone crying, "Oh, no!"* Call attention to the sound of the breaking glass and the person's sad reaction. Explain how you can infer that he or she must have dropped and broken something made of glass.

STEP FOUR Practice the Skill

Use pages 65–68. See *Teacher Note* on each page.

STEP FIVE Provide Feedback

Discuss pupils' answers. **METACOGNITION:** Ask pupils to describe what they did. You may need to ask: **What information did you use to figure out your answer?**

ENRICHMENT ACTIVITIES

Display a variety of workers' hats, or pictures of them, as well as pictures of things those workers would use on the job. For example: a nurse's cap and bandage. Have pupils match a hat and an item and identify the worker's job.

Play "What Am I?" Have pupils make up riddles about items in the classroom. For example: *I am sharp, and I cut paper. What am I?* The pupil who answers correctly gets to say the next riddle.

Take a walk with your pupils. Point out situations and ask questions such as *Why do you think that bird flew away? Why does that car have a blinking light?* Encourage pupils to give evidence for their responses.

SKILL 17 PAGES 69–72   Changes in Word Meanings

STEP ONE Define the Skill

Discuss with your pupils the meaning of understanding *changes in word meanings:* **seeing how a word can have different meanings depending on how it is used in a sentence.**

STEP TWO Identify the Steps

Explain to your pupils the steps they need to follow to understand changes in word meaning:
1. Think of the usual meaning of the word.
2. Decide whether the usual meaning is being used in the sentence.
3. If it is not, try to figure out the meaning based on the way the word is used.

STEP THREE Demonstrate the Skill

Ask pupils to watch and listen as you understand changes in word meanings. **SUGGESTION:** Write

these two sentences on the board: *My two feet are sore,* and *Stand two feet away from the door.* Define *feet* in each sentence and explain how you can tell *feet* has two different meanings in the sentences.

STEP FOUR Practice the Skill

Use pages 69–72. See *Teacher Note* on each page.

STEP FIVE Provide Feedback

Discuss pupils' answers. **METACOGNITION:** Ask pupils to describe what they did. You may need to ask: **Which sentence or picture clue did you use to figure out the meaning of the word?**

ENRICHMENT ACTIVITIES

Read *Amelia Bedelia* by Peggy Parrish. Discuss Amelia's antics as they relate to her misunderstanding of the meaning of words.

Have pupils think of ways the words *take* and *have* are used. For example: *take—take one cookie, it didn't take long, take piano lessons; have—what we will have for lunch, how much money I have, we have to go now.*

Make a list of people and their same-name activities. For example: joggers jog, builders build, bakers bake. Explain how changes in the base word change the meaning. Ask volunteers to use the word pairs in a sentence.

Analyzing

BLOOM'S TAXONOMY

KNOWLEDGE	COMPREHENSION	APPLICATION	ANALYSIS	SYNTHESIS	EVALUATION

ANALYSIS is the term used in Bloom's Taxonomy for the fourth stage in cognitive development. Analysis is the ability to break down information into its integral parts and to identify the relationship of each part to the total organization.

The authors of this program have identified the following skills as being particularly helpful in developing Bloom's fourth stage:

1. Judging Completeness
2. Thinking About Facts That Fit
3. Distinguishing Abstract from Concrete
4. Judging Logic of Actions
5. Identifying Parts of a Story
6. Examining Story Logic
7. Recognizing True and False

Step-by-step procedures for teaching each of these skills follow. These lesson plans will help you use the program with ease as you incorporate *thinking skills* into your teaching day. Enrichment activities that accompany each lesson will help your students apply their newly acquired thinking skills to a variety of situations.

After this unit has been completed, copy and distribute the School-Home Newsletter on pages T-38 and T-39.

Judging Completeness

STEP ONE Define the Skill

Discuss with your pupils the meaning of *judging completeness:* **deciding whether important information is missing from a picture or sentence.**

STEP TWO Identify the Steps

Explain to your pupils the steps they need to follow to judge completeness:
1. Look at the picture or read carefully.
2. Decide whether anything is missing.
3. Decide what is needed to make the item complete.
4. Complete the item by adding the missing parts.

STEP THREE Demonstrate the Skill

Ask pupils to watch and listen as you judge the completeness of an item, following Step Two. **SUGGESTION:** Have pupils imagine you are going to paint a picture. Lay out a cup of water, watercolors, and a paintbrush. Study the items and note that if you are going to use watercolors, you will need paper in addition to the paint. Your materials are not complete unless you have everything you need to paint.

STEP FOUR Practice the Skill

Use pages 76–78. See *Teacher Note* on each page.

STEP FIVE Provide Feedback

Discuss pupils' answers. **METACOGNITION:** Ask pupils to describe what they did. You may need to ask: **How could you tell the item was incomplete? How did you decide which part was needed to complete each picture? How did you decide which word was missing to complete the sentence?**

ENRICHMENT ACTIVITIES

Have pupils make a mural of the "Without Family." They could live in a house without windows, ride bikes without pedals, fly kites without string, or walk the dog without a leash. Have each pupil contribute to the mural.

Tell pupils to pretend a special event is coming up. Have them write invitations and ask a partner to check carefully to see that they have included all the important information.

Have pupils observe five or six items and then turn their back to the display. Secretly remove an item and rearrange the remaining items. Have pupils determine which item is missing.

Thinking About Facts That Fit

STEP ONE Define the Skill

Discuss with your pupils the meaning of *thinking about facts that fit:* **deciding whether an object or idea goes with another object or idea.**

STEP TWO Identify the Steps

Explain to your pupils the steps they need to follow to think about whether a fact fits:
1. Identify the main idea.
2. Read the facts or look at the objects.
3. Decide whether each fact or object belongs with the main idea.

STEP THREE Demonstrate the Skill

Ask pupils to watch and listen as you decide whether or not some facts fit, following Step Two. **SUGGESTION:** Tell pupils you are going to write a paragraph about a very good friend. List these facts on the board—*my friend's name, other friends' names, why I like my friend, what we do together, where we live.* Decide which facts should be included because they fit with the main idea—the friend's name, why you like him or her, where you both live, and what you do together—and which fact should not be included because it doesn't fit—other friends' names.

STEP FOUR Practice the Skill

Use pages 79–80. See *Teacher Note* on each page.

STEP FIVE Provide Feedback

Discuss pupils' answers. **METACOGNITION:** Ask pupils to describe what they did. You may need to ask: **How did you decide which facts were most important?**

ENRICHMENT ACTIVITIES

Assign a topic or category to "Word Wizard" groups and have the groups list appropriate words. For example: if the topic is a short vowel/long vowel with silent *e*, the Word Wizard group might suggest the words *hop/hope*. Post the lists and challenge pupils to write two sentences using a word pair.

Make a bulletin-board train. Write a heading on a "puff of smoke," such as *Words of Cheer*. Have pupils write their ideas about your title on strips of paper and load them into a car. Change the heading every day.

Have volunteers select a simple item from home and prepare a sales talk about the item to present to their classmates. After the presentation, have listeners tell what facts they learned about the item.

SKILL 20 PAGES 81–84

Abstract or Concrete

STEP ONE Define the Skill

Discuss with your pupils the meaning of deciding between *abstract or concrete:* **knowing the difference between things that can be seen or touched and things that can only be thought about.**

STEP TWO Identify the Steps

Explain to your pupils the steps they need to follow to decide between abstract or concrete:
1. Read carefully.
2. Place items that you can see, touch, taste, smell, or hear in one group.
3. Place items that you can only think about, such as feelings or ideas, in another group.

STEP THREE Demonstrate the Skill

Ask pupils to watch and listen as you decide whether a term is abstract or concrete, following Step Two. **SUGGESTION:** List on the board various words having to do with school—for example, *bell,*

learning, clock, chalkboard, thought, math, book, door. Read each word aloud and ask whether it can be seen, touched, tasted, smelled, or heard; if so, circle it. If it can only be thought about, draw a box around it. Then challenge pupils to list concrete or abstract words on a subject or topic that interests them, such as *weather* or *animals.*

STEP FOUR Practice the Skill

Use pages 81–84. See *Teacher Note* on each page.

STEP FIVE Provide Feedback

Discuss pupils' answers. **METACOGNITION:** Ask pupils to describe what they did. You may need to ask: **How did you decide if you could see, hear, touch, smell, or taste something? How did you decide if you could only think about it?**

ENRICHMENT ACTIVITIES

Write several sentences on the board, underlining some of the words. For example: *The baby is cute. Kevin has a smart dog.* Have pupils tell which underlined words stand for things that can be touched and which stand for things that cannot be touched.

Make a list of intangibles and have pupils match each one with a specific action. For example: *praise*—a pat on the back; *friendship*—a high five; *fun*—skipping arm-in-arm.

Build a word web of concrete examples around the abstract word *love*. For example, pupils may suggest words such as *hug, kiss, heart, smile*. Follow a similar procedure to build a word web for the word *fun*.

Logic of Actions

STEP ONE Define the Skill

Discuss with your pupils the meaning of judging *logic of actions:* **deciding whether you think an action makes sense.**

STEP TWO Identify the Steps

Explain to your pupils the steps they need to follow to judge the logic of actions:
1. Figure out what the situation is.
2. Think of several actions you could take in that situation.
3. Choose the actions that make sense.

STEP THREE Demonstrate the Skill

Ask pupils to watch and listen as you judge the logic of actions, following Step Two. **SUGGESTION:** Write these two problem situations on the board, with the two alternative actions as multiple choice options—*If I want to get down the street in a hurry, I (run/take) the bus. If I want to get across town in a hurry, I (run/take) the bus.* Choose the action that makes better sense in each situation and explain why.

STEP FOUR Practice the Skill

Use pages 85–88. See *Teacher Note* on each page.

STEP FIVE Provide Feedback

Discuss pupils' answers. **METACOGNITION:** Ask pupils to describe what they did. You may need to ask: **How did you decide what made sense to use in each situation?**

E N R I C H M E N T   A C T I V I T I E S

Ask pupils to explain the logic behind some of their actions at school. For example, you might ask: *What made you let Ben go in front of you? What made you give me this nice picture? What made you think Seth needed green paint?*

List pupils' favorite activities. Have each pupil make a picture of items or conditions necessary to do their favorite activity. Post the pictures. Then read one activity at a time and ask pupils to select the picture that fits that activity.

Read the book *Franklin in the Dark* by Paulette Bourgeois. Discuss the logic of Franklin's solution to his problem and the logic of others' offers.

Parts of a Story

STEP ONE Define the Skill

Discuss with your pupils the meaning of identifying the *parts of a story:* **identifying the characters, the setting, and the action (plot).**

STEP TWO Identify the Steps

Explain to your pupils the steps they need to follow to identify the parts of a story:
1. Read the story.
2. Find the characters—the people or animals in the story.
3. Decide the setting—where the story takes place.
4. Describe the action that takes place.

STEP THREE Demonstrate the Skill

Ask pupils to watch and listen as you identify the parts of a story, following Step Two.

SUGGESTION: Read *Jack and the Beanstalk* aloud. Explain to pupils that Jack and the giant are the main characters. The setting is the make-believe land of the giant. The action concerns Jack's attempt to outwit the giant.

STEP FOUR Practice the Skill

Use pages 89–90. See *Teacher Note* on each page.

STEP FIVE Provide Feedback

Discuss pupils' answers. **METACOGNITION:** Ask pupils to describe what they did. You may need to ask: **How did you pick out the characters? How did you figure out the setting? How did you follow along with the action of the story?**

Have volunteers "stand in" as the actual authors of their favorite books. Other pupils could tell what they like about the stories and ask questions about characters, dialogue, setting, or outcome.

With a group of pupils, read *Mary Wore Her Red Dress* by Merle Peek. Then have pupils tell the more complete story that is shown in the illustrations but is not included in the text.

Read aloud a familiar fairy tale. Then, as a group, list the main characters, the setting, and the plot. Have pupils use the list to write a modified version of the fairy tale.

SKILL 23 PAGES 91–92

Story Logic

STEP ONE Define the Skill

Discuss with your pupils the meaning of judging *story logic:* telling whether events in a story are about the main idea and whether they follow the right order.

STEP TWO Identify the Steps

Explain to your pupils the steps they need to follow to judge the logic of a story:
1. Determine the main idea of the story.
2. Ask yourself if each sentence really is about the main idea.
3. Decide whether the ideas or events are in the right order.

STEP THREE Demonstrate the Skill

Ask pupils to watch and listen as you judge the logic of a short paragraph, following Step Two. **SUGGESTION:** Write the following paragraph on the board—*Matt and his dad went on the roller coaster.*

Matt's dad took him to the amusement park. They played games. Matt's dad won a big stuffed animal. It wasn't Dad's birthday. Explain that the main idea is Matt's day at the amusement park. The second sentence should come first; it begins the day at the amusement park. The fifth sentence should be dropped; it doesn't belong because it doesn't have anything to do with the trip to the amusement park. Rewrite the paragraph correctly.

STEP FOUR Practice the Skill

Use pages 91–92. See *Teacher Note* on each page.

STEP FIVE Provide Feedback

Discuss pupils' answers. **METACOGNITION:** Ask pupils to describe what they did. You may need to ask: **What clues did you use to figure out the order of the events? How did you know which words to choose to complete each sentence in the story?**

Have pupils choose a comic strip from some old newspapers you provide. Challenge pupils to cut apart the comic strips, mix them up, and then rearrange the frames into logical order.

Provide small groups with a common object, such as a coin, a milk carton, or a yardstick. Direct them to write three sentences about their object. Two of the sentences should be connected, and one should not fit. Partners should identify the sentence that does not fit.

At the end of a school day, write a group story on sentence strips about the day's events. Be sure to include words such as *then, before,* and *after.* Mix up the strips and have pupils put the sentences back together in logical order the following day.

STEP ONE Define the Skill

Discuss with your pupils the meaning of *recognizing true and false:* **telling when information is always correct or sometimes incorrect.**

STEP TWO Identify the Steps

Explain to your pupils the steps they need to follow in order to recognize whether a sentence is true or false:
1. Read the sentence.
2. Look for words such as *all* or *none* that may be a clue the statement is not always true.
3. Decide how a false sentence may be changed to a true one.

STEP THREE Demonstrate the Skill

Ask pupils to watch and listen as you recognize true and false, following Step Two. **SUGGESTION:** Write two sentences on the board—*Some children have brown eyes,* and *All children have black hair.* Read the first sentence aloud and explain that it is true because some children do have brown eyes. Then read the second sentence aloud and explain that it is false because some children have brown, blond, or red hair. Explain that the sentence could be changed to a true one by beginning the sentence with the word *Some* instead of *All.*

STEP FOUR Practice the Skill

Use pages 93–94. See *Teacher Note* on each page.

STEP FIVE Provide Feedback

Discuss pupils' answers. **METACOGNITION:** Ask pupils to describe what they did. You may need to ask: **How did you decide which sentences were not true? How did you figure out which word could be changed to make the sentence true?**

ENRICHMENT ACTIVITIES

Play a game in which pupils raise their right hand to identify a true statement and cover their ears to identify a false statement.

Make a "True or False Red Alert" bulletin board. Put the words *never, always, none, all, any,* and *only* on a red background. When pupils hear false statements using these words, they should call a "red alert" and identify the word or words on the board.

Read the story *Franklin Fibs* by Paulette Bourgeois. Discuss the fibs told by Franklin and how his friends knew they were not true. Invite volunteers to discuss why telling a fib is not a good idea.

Class Assessment Summary

TEACHER

SCHOOL

GRADE

Directions: Daily observation and planned activities help determine whether students have achieved mastery of a particular skill. Indicate each student's mastery of a skill by writing the date in the corresponding box.

NAMES	SKILLS ▶	1 Classifying	2 Real and Make-Believe	3 Fact and Opinion	4 Definition and Example	5 Outlining and Summarizing	6 Comparing and Contrasting	7 Identifying Structure	8 Steps in a Process	9 Understanding Pictures	10 Comparing Word Meanings	11 Identifying Main Ideas	12 Identifying Relationships

UNIT 1: KNOWING

UNIT 2: UNDERSTANDING

Class Assessment Summary

Steck-Vaughn grants permission to duplicate this page. © 1993 Steck-Vaughn Company

TEACHER

SCHOOL

GRADE

Directions: Daily observation and planned activities help determine whether students have achieved mastery of a particular skill. Indicate each student's mastery of a skill by writing the date in the corresponding box.

NAMES	SKILLS▸											
		13	14	15	16	17	18	19	20	21	22	23	24

UNIT 3: APPLYING

UNIT 4: ANALYZING

- 13 Ordering Objects
- 14 Estimating
- 15 Thinking About What Will Happen
- 16 Inferring
- 17 Changes in Word Meanings
- 18 Judging Completeness
- 19 Thinking About Facts That Fit
- 20 Abstract or Concrete
- 21 Logic of Actions
- 22 Parts of a Story
- 23 Story Logic
- 24 Recognizing True and False

Thinker's Corner

SCHOOL–HOME NEWSLETTER

UNIT 1
KNOWING

In the first unit of *Critical Thinking: Reading, Thinking, and Reasoning Skills,* your child has been studying the following skills:

- classifying
- real and make-believe
- fact and opinion
- definition and example
- outlining and summarizing

This newsletter is designed to provide an important link between home and school. You can support your child's learning habits by asking what he or she has learned in school and by discussing papers brought home. You may also wish to do some of the activities suggested in this newsletter.

Fill the Closet

This activity can help your child practice classifying. Use old magazines or catalogs. Divide a sheet of paper into three sections: top, middle, and bottom. Tell your child this is a closet. Things that are worn on the head, such as hats and scarves, belong on the top shelf. Things that are worn on the body, such as shirts, pants, or dresses, go on the middle shelf. Things that are worn on the feet, such as shoes or boots, go on the bottom shelf. Have your child cut out pictures of items and glue them on the appropriate "shelf."

Real? Or Make-Believe?

Draw a line down the center of a sheet of paper. On one side write *Real,* on the other side write *Make-Believe*. As you look through old magazines with your child, discuss which pictures show real people or animals and which pictures show make-believe characters. Have your child cut out the pictures and glue them in the appropriate place on the sheet of paper.

What's Your Opinion?

Help your child understand the difference between fact and opinion by asking him or her to conduct a survey. The survey could ask a question such as *How do you feel about biking*? Your child should record each person's opinion. Then have your child list some facts about the topic.

What Did You Find Out?

Every time you ask your child to tell about his or her school day, you are helping your child practice summarizing. Ask your child to tell about the survey he or she just conducted in the activity above. If necessary, remind your child to give a brief summarizing statement of each person's opinions.

Word Web

A word web can help your child understand word definitions and examples. Work with your child to complete the word web called "Super Sandcastles." Around the word *sandcastle*, write other words that describe sandcastle.

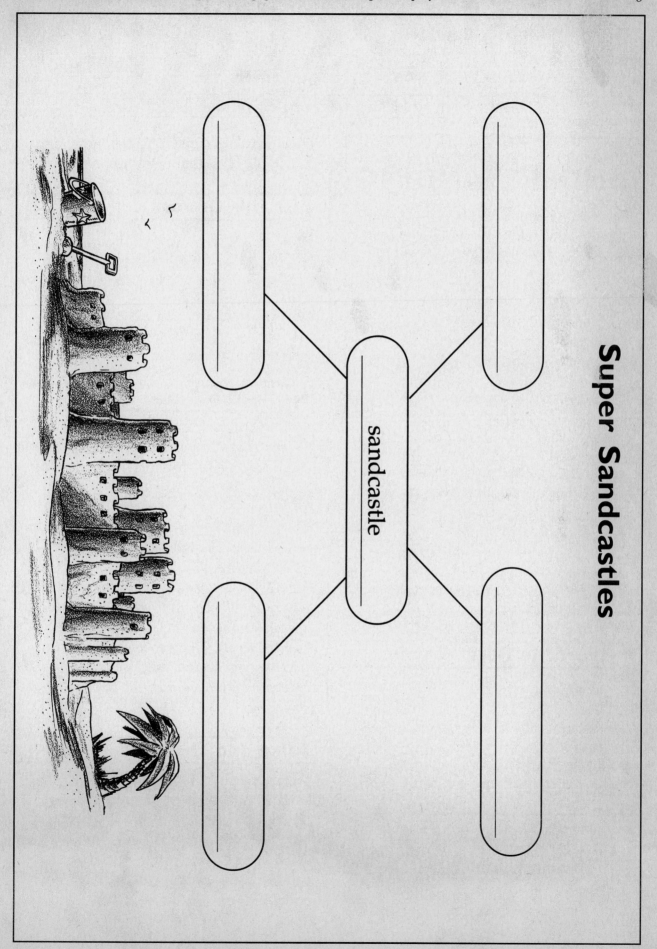

Super Sandcastles

sandcastle

Thinker's Corner

SCHOOL—HOME NEWSLETTER

UNIT 2
UNDERSTANDING

In the second unit of *Critical Thinking: Reading, Thinking, and Reasoning Skills*, your child has been studying the following skills:

- comparing and contrasting
- identifying structure
- steps in a process
- understanding pictures
- comparing word meanings
- identifying main ideas
- identifying relationships

This newsletter is designed to provide an important link between home and school. You can support your child's learning habits by asking what he or she has learned in school and by discussing papers brought home. You may also wish to do some of the activities suggested in this newsletter.

My Favorite Recipes

Ask your child to write the steps in making one of his or her favorite foods. Suggest that words such as *first*, *next*, and *last* be used in the "recipes." Your child might want to make a collection of favorites and put them in a book.

Shape City

Draw a circle, a square, a triangle, and a rectangle. Ask your child to draw a city scene using only these shapes. Encourage creativity. For example, a rectangle, a square, and two circles make a bus. Your child may enjoy coloring the scene and sharing it with family or friends.

Just the Opposite

A game of opposites can help your child compare word meanings. Draw a line down the middle of a sheet of paper. In the first column, write *up, big, fast*, and *tall*. Ask your child to write the word that means the opposite of each listed word (*down, little, slow, short*).

Name the Title

Titles of stories and books often reveal the main idea of the story. Help your child practice identifying main ideas by asking him or her to suggest several titles for the following paragraph:

The little puppy went on a picnic with his family. The girl in the family threw a ball at the puppy. The ball rolled into high weeds. The puppy ran after it. The weeds were so tall. The puppy found the ball, but he didn't know which way to go to get out of the weeds. First he ran one way. Then he ran another. He was lost in the weeds! Soon he heard the girl call. He ran toward the voice.

Alike and Different

Ask your child to name kinds of pets, such as cats, dogs, birds, and fish. Discuss how the animals are alike, how they are different, and which animal your child prefers. Then ask your child to complete the comparison activity "Cat and Dog."

Steck-Vaughn grants permission to duplicate this page. © 1993 Steck-Vaughn Company

Cat and Dog

How Are They Alike?

_____

_____

_____

_____

_____

_____

How Are They Different?

cat	dog

Thinker's Corner

SCHOOL–HOME NEWSLETTER

UNIT 3
APPLYING

In the third unit of *Critical Thinking: Reading, Thinking, and Reasoning Skills,* your child has been studying the following skills:

- ordering objects
- estimating
- thinking about what will happen
- inferring
- changes in word meanings

This newsletter is designed to provide an important link between home and school. You can support your child's learning habits by asking what he or she has learned in school and by discussing papers brought home. You may also wish to do some of the activities suggested in this newsletter.

Complete the Pattern

Help your child practice ordering objects by asking your child what would come next in each of the patterns below.

1   3   5   7   9   11

C   D   C   D   C   D

△ ○ ○   △ ○ ○

+   + +   + + +

What If?

To practice anticipating possibilities, ask your child to think about what would happen if—
1. *It started raining hamburgers.*
2. *You won a free vacation to Hawaii.*
3. *Your family lived on the moon.*
4. *The whole school went on a field trip.*

Which Room Am I In?

Help your child practice inferring by asking him or her to identify which room you are describing in each of the following sentences:
1. *I'm sitting on the bed reading.*
2. *It's morning, and I am brushing my teeth.*
3. *I put some dishes into the sink.*
4. *I'll turn off the TV.*

More Than One Meaning

Ask your child to answer the following questions:
1. *What kind of fly buzzes around and bothers you?* (an insect)
2. *What kind of fly do you hit when you're in a ball game ?* (a fly ball—one that goes high up in the air)
3. *What kind of fly do you do on an airplane?* (to ride in the air)

How Many?

The activity "How Many Baseballs?" will help your child practice estimating. After your child completes the page, ask how he or she figured out each estimate. If necessary, cut out the baseballs and place them in the box to verify the accuracy of the estimate.

Steck-Vaughn grants permission to duplicate this page. © 1993 Steck-Vaughn Company

How Many Baseballs?

Look at the baseball in the box. How many more baseballs do you think will fill the box? Draw a circle around the group of baseballs that will fill the box.

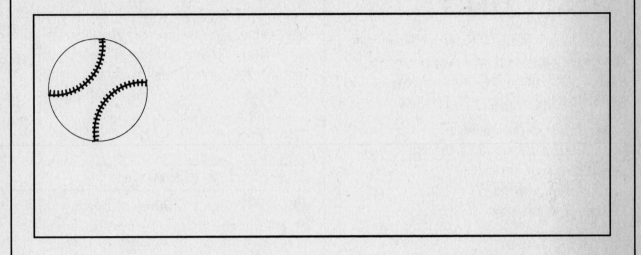

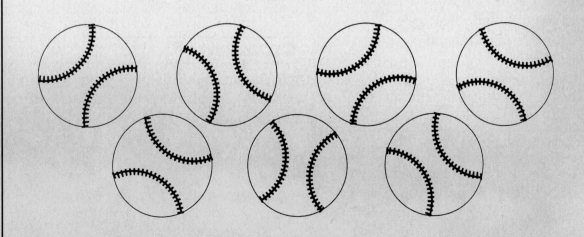

Thinker's Corner

UNIT 4
ANALYZING

In the fourth unit of *Critical Thinking: Reading, Thinking, and Reasoning Skills*, your child has been studying the following skills:

- judging completeness
- thinking about facts that fit
- abstract or concrete
- logic of actions
- parts of a story
- story logic
- recognizing true and false

This newsletter is designed to provide an important link between home and school. You can support your child's learning habits by asking what he or she has learned in school and by discussing papers brought home. You may also wish to do some of the activities suggested in this newsletter.

What Rhymes?

Have your child work with judging completeness by asking him or her to complete the following rhymes:

1. *On the way to town I met a pig.*
   The pig and I, we danced a ___.
2. *On the way to town I met a cat.*
   Fancy that, a cat with a ___.

Information Please

Discuss relevance of information with your child by asking him or her to list some important things to do in an emergency. Teach your child how to notify emergency personnel in your area. Then list important information to give. For example, *Do you need to tell where you live?* (yes); *Do you need to give your birth date?* (no); *Do you need to tell what the problem is?* (yes). Stress with your child the importance of staying on the line until the contact tells him or her to disconnect.

If I Had a Hammer

Discuss logic of actions with your child by asking the following questions:

1. *If I had a hammer, would I be baking a cake?*
2. *If I had scissors, would I be going shopping?*

Be an Author

Use the elements of a selection to help your child write a story. Ask your child to think of some *characters* in a *place*, such as toys in a store window. Now ask him or her to think of a *problem* the characters have, such as toys wanting to get into a home. Once the *solution* is figured out, your child is ready to write the story. Have fun and encourage creative thinking!

Crossword Puzzle

Help your child distinguish between concrete and abstract words by asking him or her to fill in the crossword puzzle "Crossword Fun." The words in the ACROSS column are things you can see and touch. The words in the DOWN column describe things you cannot see or touch.

Steck-Vaughn grants permission to duplicate this page. © 1993 Steck-Vaughn Company

Crossword Fun

ACROSS

2. You wear this on your head or around your neck.
3. This is a two-wheeled riding machine.
6. You write with this.

DOWN

1. Animals might feel _____ in the hot, afternoon sun.
4. To answer a riddle, you must be very _____.
5. When you act funny and make people laugh, you are being _____.

ACROSS   DOWN
2. scarf   1. lazy
3. bicycle   4. clever
6. pencil   5. silly

STECK-VAUGHN
CRITICAL THINKING

Reading, Thinking, and Reasoning Skills

Authors

Don Barnes
Professor of Education
Ball State University; Muncie, Indiana

Arlene Burgdorf
Former Resource Consultant
Hammond Indiana Public Schools

L. Stanley Wenck
Professor of Educational Psychology
Ball State University; Muncie, Indiana

Consultant

Gloria Sesso
Supervisor of Social Studies
Half Hollow Hills School District; Dix Hills, New York

LEVEL

| A | B | C | D | E | F |

STECK-VAUGHN
C O M P A N Y
A Subsidiary of National Education Corporation

ACKNOWLEDGMENTS

Executive Editor: Elizabeth Strauss

Project Editor: Anita Arndt

Consulting Editor: Melinda Veatch

Design, Production, and Editorial Services: The Quarasan Group, Inc.

Contributing Writers: Tara McCarthy
Linda Ward Beech

Cover Design: Linda Adkins Graphic Design

Text:
Every effort has been made to trace the ownership of all copyrighted material and to secure the necessary permission to reprint these selections. In the event of any question arising as to the use of any material, the editor and publisher, while expressing regret for any inadvertent error, will be happy to make the necessary correction in future printings.

"One, one Cinnamon bun" reprinted with permission of Philomel Books and Curtis Brown, Ltd. from CATCH ME & KISS ME & SAY IT AGAIN, text © 1978 by Clyde Watson.

"Pie Problem" (p. 164) from A LIGHT IN THE ATTIC by Shel Silverstein. Copyright © 1981 by Evil Eye Music, Inc. Reprinted with permission of HarperCollins and Edite Kroll Literary Agency.

"thrickle" reprinted with permission of Moffitt-Lee Productions and Macmillan Publishing Company from SNIGLETS by Rich Hall and Friends. Copyright © 1984 by Not the Network Company, Inc.

Photography:
p. 5 — Nita Winter
p. 28 — D. Gordon/The Image Bank West
p. 29 — Rick Reinhard
p. 53 — Nita Winter
p. 75 — H. Armstrong Roberts

Illustration:
pp. 6, 7, 23, 48, — Linda Hawkins
pp. 8, 12, 13, 15, 16, 20, 21, 26, 33, 41, 42, 44, 50, 57, 62, 63, 66, 68, 70, 88, 90, 92 — Scott Bieser
pp. 9, 19, 22, 25, 32, 39, 43, 46, 49, 56, 59, 76, 81, 86, 91, 94 — Lynn McClain
pp. 10, 82, 93 — Peg Dougherty
pp. 11, 18, 24, 27, 28, 35, 45, 51, 52, 58, 61, 65, 71, 73, 74, 95, 96, — Kenneth Smith
pp. 14, 17, 37, 47, 69, 77 — Bill Ogden
pp. 36, 85 — Nancy Walter
pp. 38, 60, 78, — Elizabeth Allen

ISBN 0–8114–6601–9

TABLE OF CONTENTS

TABLE OF CONTENTS

Knowing

Teacher Note
In order to develop Bloom's first stage—knowing—the pupil needs to engage in the following skills:
- Classifying
- Discriminating Between Real and Make-Believe
- Discriminating Between Fact and Opinion
- Discriminating Between Definition and Example
- Outlining and Summarizing

Knowing means getting the facts together. Let's try it out. Look at the girl in the picture. Do you think she's happy? Why or why not? Is she smiling? How can you tell?

Classifying

Find the pictures of two things that belong in each box. Write their letters on the lines in the box.

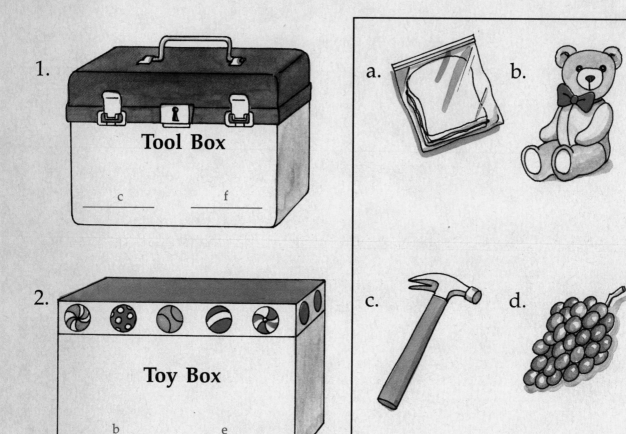

1. Tool Box
   c _____ f _____

a. b.

2. Toy Box
   b _____ e _____

c. d.

3. Lunch Box
   a _____ d _____

e. f.

Critical Thinking, Level B © 1993 Steck-Vaughn

Name

_____

Teacher Note
After pupils have completed the page, ask them to name other objects that belong in each of the boxes shown. You may wish to extend the activity by challenging pupils to name what belongs in each of the following boxes: school pencil box, sewing box, tackle box.

Classifying

Look at each numbered picture on the left. Find two pictures on the right that show something like it. Write their names on the lines.

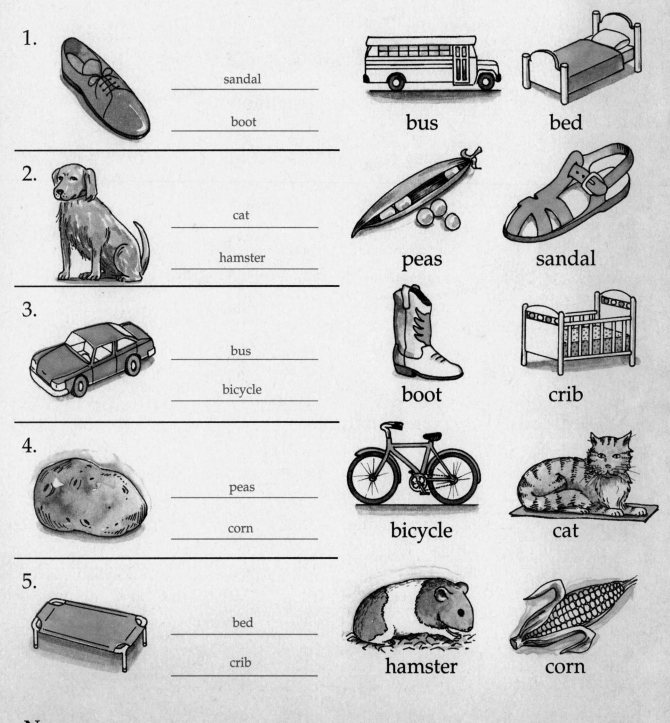

1. sandal

   boot

   bus   bed

2. cat

   hamster

   peas   sandal

3. bus

   bicycle

   boot   crib

4. peas

   corn

   bicycle   cat

5. bed

   crib

   hamster   corn

Name

Teacher Note
When pupils have finished, ask them to explain how the items in each group are the same. You may wish to have them name other items that could belong to each group.

Classifying

Where can you find the things written on the fish? Write each word under the hook that tells where each thing should go.

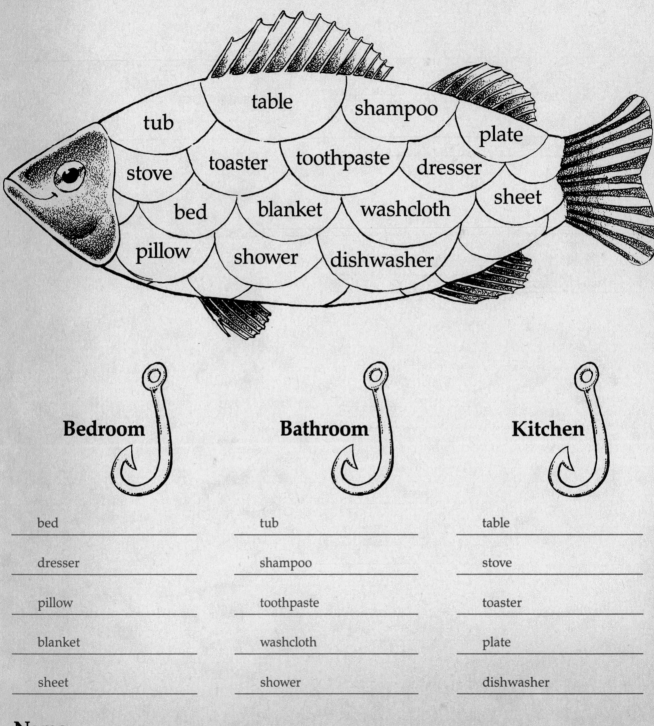

Bedroom	Bathroom	Kitchen
bed	tub	table
dresser	shampoo	stove
pillow	toothpaste	toaster
blanket	washcloth	plate
sheet	shower	dishwasher

Name _____

Critical Thinking, Level B © 1993 Steck-Vaughn

Teacher Note
Read the directions and the other words on the page to pupils, but allow them to complete the page independently. When you discuss their answers, ask pupils to think of other items that can be found in these rooms.

Read each sentence. Find the word in the **Word Box** that fits in the blank. Write the letter of that word.

Word Box

A. bug	B. dish	C. car	D. numbers
E. clothing	F. toy	G. meat	H. fruit

1. A  is one of a group of __D__ .

2. A is a kind of __G__ .

3. A is a kind of __H__ .

4. A is a kind of __A__ .

5. A is a kind of __C__ .

6. A (bowl) is a kind of __B__ .

7. A (egg toy) is a kind of __F__ .

8. A (sock) is a kind of __E__ .

Name _____

Teacher Note
Read the directions to pupils and allow them to work independently. After pupils have completed the page, select some of the categories and ask pupils to name other items that could be included.

Find the two words that go with each picture. Write the letters of the two words on the lines.

1. A. bird
   B. chair
   C. top
   D. robin
   E. poodle
   F. furniture
   G. toy
   H. dog
   I. clothes
   J. jacket

2. A. tulip
   B. cat
   C. apple
   D. jewelry
   E. flower
   F. house
   G. fruit
   H. building
   I. animal
   J. ring

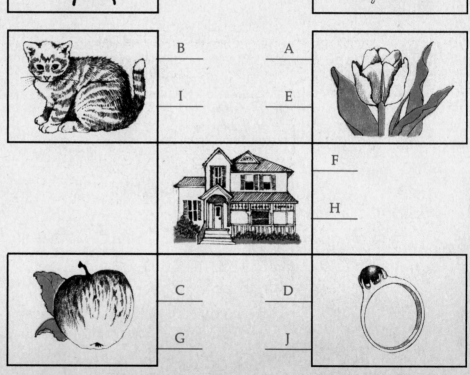

Name _____

Critical Thinking, Level B © 1993 Steck-Vaughn

Teacher Note
Read the directions and allow pupils to work independently. When pupils complete the page, ask them to give their answers in complete sentences—for example, *A robin is a kind of bird*.

10

Circle the sentences that tell about something make-believe.
Put an **X** on the picture that shows something real.

1. (Horses go to bed when they are sick.)
2. (Some trees grow upside down.)
3. (Some pigs have five legs and a cap.)
4. A man and a boy can row a boat.
5. (A squirrel can row a boat.)

Name _____

Teacher Note
Read the directions and the sentences to pupils. When they have completed the page, ask them to change the make-believe sentences so that they tell something real. For example, *Horses go to bed when they are sick* could become *Horses should not be ridden when they are sick.*

11

Real and Make-Believe

Put an **R** before the things that are real. Put an **M** before the things that are make-believe.

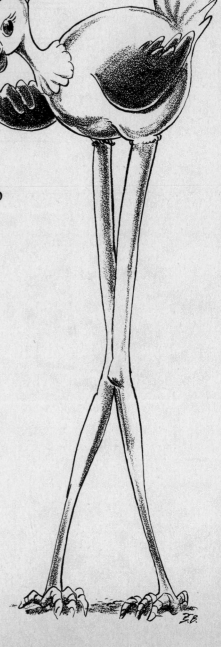

M ____ 1. a fairy godmother

R ____ 2. a plant with thorns

R ____ 3. a brown lizard

M ____ 4. a purple leopard

M ____ 5. a hen with legs four feet long

M ____ 6. a pencil that writes with no help

R ____ 7. a brown-and-white spotted cow

M ____ 8. a dancing pig

M ____ 9. a magic wand

M ____ 10. a twenty-foot tall giant

M ____ 11. orange raindrops

M ____ 12. a cow that flies without a plane

R ____ 13. a white rose

M ____ 14. a three-foot-high apple

R ____ 15. a chair that stays outside

Name _____

Critical Thinking, Level B © 1993 Steck-Vaughn

Teacher Note
Before pupils begin the page, discuss whether the hen in the picture is real or make-believe. Have pupils explain reasons for their responses.

Write **M** if the sentence tells something make-believe. Write **R** if it tells something real. Then match each sentence on the left to one on the right that tells about the same thing.

__**M**__　1. A giant scared Sam.

__M__　2. Mice paint houses.

__M__　3. The pumpkin sang.

__M__　4. I play with an elf.

__R__　5. The frog jumped.

__R__　6. Juan watched a game.

__R__　7. A dog barks at me.

__R__　8. Stars shine at night.

__R__　9. He bought a pan.

__M__　10. Our cat washes cars.

A. A frog became a prince.

B. We like pumpkin pie.

C. Stars fell on his head.

D. Giants are in the story.

E. The dog danced a polka.

F. Juan saw three goblins.

G. A cat washes its face.

H. Mice run in old houses.

I. The pan laughed loudly.

J. An elf was in my dream.

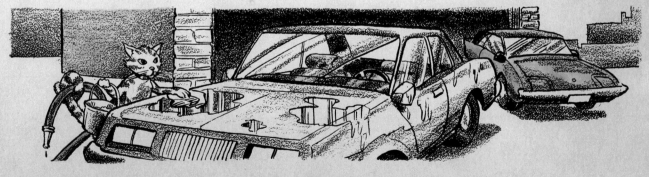

Name
_____

Teacher Note
Complete the first item with pupils to be sure they understand the directions. It may also be helpful to introduce the words *pumpkin*, *polka*, and *goblins* before pupils begin working independently.

Real and Make-Believe

Ann

These children like
to tell stories. Ann
tells stories about things
that really can happen.
Mike likes to tell
make-believe stories.

Mike

Copy each sentence below under the correct heading.

I saw a purple dog.
My sister tells funny stories.
My lizard has four legs.

My house is made of
peanut butter.
I often drink milk
while eating.
A sock gets hungry
at lunchtime.

Real	**Make-believe**
My sister tells funny stories.	I saw a purple dog.
My lizard has four legs.	My house is made of peanut butter.
I often drink milk while eating.	A sock gets hungry at lunchtime.

Name

Teacher Note
Read the story about Ann and Mike with pupils. Then read each sentence and have students tell you whether
Ann or Mike might have said it. Students may then copy each sentence under the correct heading.

Fact and Opinion

Write **F** before each sentence that tells a fact. Write **O** before each sentence that tells an opinion.

_F_   1. Rabbits run faster than turtles.

_F_   2. Pencils are used for writing.

_O_   3. This peach is the best peach in the world.

_O_   4. Climbing trees is not a good thing to do.

_F_   5. Dinosaurs lived long ago.

_O_   6. My kitten is prettier than your kitten.

_F_   7. Babies are smaller than mothers.

_O_   8. That juice is too sweet.

_F_   9. Hammers and saws are tools.

_F_   10. Some shoes are made of leather.

_O_   11. Bananas taste better than apples.

_O_   12. Cats are not as friendly as dogs.

_F_   13. There are many different kinds of cars.

_O_   14. That barn is too big and ugly.

_O_   15. Rob's picture is better than mine.

Name

Teacher Note

Before pupils begin, have them give their definitions of *fact* and *opinion*. Let them complete the page independently. When they have finished, have them change some of the opinion sentences to facts—for example, *This peach is the best peach in the world* could become *This peach grew on our tree*.

A. Draw a line from each fact sentence to an opinion sentence on the same subject.

Facts

1. Most people have hair.
2. Thanksgiving is a holiday.
3. Horses have four legs.
4. People need food.
5. Baseball is a game.
6. Bicycles have wheels.
7. A blue jay is a bird.
8. My mom drives to work.

Opinions

A. Riding a horse is dangerous.
B. Lunch is the best meal of the day.
C. Bluejays are too noisy.
D. Red hair is the most beautiful.
E. Everyone should have a bicycle.
F. It's easy to drive a car.
G. Thanksgiving is the best day of all.
H. The rules of baseball are easy.

B. Look at the hat.
Then write two sentences of your own.

1. A **fact** about the hat:

   Answers will vary.

2. My **opinion** about the hat:

Name

Teacher Note
Before pupils begin the page, discuss the difference between a *fact* and an *opinion*. Ask pupils to give examples of each. When they have completed the page, ask pupils to read aloud their sentences for part B. Classmates should judge whether each sentence is a fact or an opinion.

Read the story. Underline the three sentences that tell opinions.

   Our class gave a Book Fair. We set up booths in the hallway. Each booth was for a different kind of book. <u>I think the mystery story booth was the most interesting.</u>
   We made posters and signs for our Book Fair. <u>I think my poster was the best one.</u> Carol and Mike painted a sign that was bigger than any of the others.
   Every class in the school visited the fair. <u>It was the best Book Fair in the whole wide world!</u>

Name

Teacher Note
Explain that most stories are a mixture of fact and opinion. Ask pupils to think of television commercials they have heard. Have them discuss which parts of these commercials are facts and which are opinions. After reading the story with the pupils, have them complete the page independently.

Finish the two sentences beside each picture. Make one sentence tell a fact. Make the other sentence tell your opinion.

Fact: The riders _Sentences will vary._

Opinion: Biking is _____

Fact: The girls _____

Opinion: Jumping is _____

Fact: The boys _____

Opinion: I think _____

Fact: The children _____

Opinion: Camping is _____

Name _____

Critical Thinking, Level B © 1993 Steck-Vaughn

Teacher Note
Allow time for individual work. When pupils have finished, ask them to read aloud their sentences.
Emphasize that while they may easily agree on the facts, they are less likely to do so with the opinions.

A. On each line, write the number of the correct word from the **Word Box**.

Word Box

_____4_____ grows on a tree

_____1_____ lives but is not a plant

_____2_____ holds many things inside

_____5_____ holds water and other drinks

_____3_____ something to play with

1. animal
2. box
3. toy
4. leaf
5. cup

B. Which word in the Word Box goes with each picture? Write the number of the word on the line.

_____3_____

_____4_____

_____2_____

_____1_____

_____5_____

Name

_____

Teacher Note
Discuss the difference between *definition* and *example*. A *definition* often describes a group of things—a toy can be defined as something you play with. An *example* of a toy is a doll. Have pupils complete part A and discuss answers with them. Then have them finish part B independently.

Definition and Example

A. On each line, write the number of the correct word from the **Word Box**.

Word Box

<u> 3 </u> These are growing things with leaves.

<u> 2 </u> These are part of the alphabet.

<u> 4 </u> You stay in them.

<u> 1 </u> It helps you to grow.

1. food
2. letters
3. plants
4. buildings

B. On each line, write the number of a word from the Word Box. You will use each number more than once.

2   3   4   1

1   4   2   3

Name

Teacher Note
Before pupils begin, read the words in the Word Box with them. When they have completed the exercise, tell them that the sentences in part A are definitions which describe the Word Box words. The pictures in part B are examples of those definitions.

Read each definition and the examples. Circle the word that names the example shown in the picture.

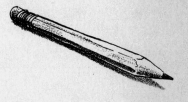

1. a covering for the head

scarf
(hat)
helmet

2. an animal with wings

butterfly
bird
(bat)

3. a tool for writing

crayon
(pencil)
pen

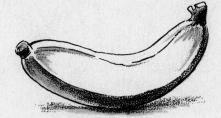

4. a round toy

(yoyo)
marble
ball

5. a yellow fruit

(banana)
lemon
pear

6. a sea animal

seal
fish
(dolphin)

Name _____

Teacher Note
Have pupils complete the page independently. Discuss their answers. Then have them choose objects in the classroom and make their own definitions.

Read the word under each picture. Write the word under the correct definition.

1. a tool for writing

   pencil

   pen

   crayon

2. a tool used by builders

   hammer

   nail

   saw

3. a bird that can swim

   swan

   duck

   pelican

swan

hammer

pencil

duck

nail

saw

pen

crayon

pelican

Critical Thinking, Level B © 1993 Steck-Vaughn

Name

Teacher Note
After pupils have finished the exercise independently, have them name other examples of each definition. You might divide the class into two groups and have a contest to see which group can name the most examples under each definition.

22

Look at the two clowns. Write words from the box to tell about each clown.

| big hat |
| happy face |
| big pants |
| short |
| tall |
| no hair |
| sad face |
| tiny hat |
| small coat |
| curly hair |

Bud the Clown

1. _____short_____

2. _____happy face_____

3. _____tiny hat_____

4. _____small coat_____

5. _____no hair_____

Babs the Clown

1. _____tall_____

2. _____sad face_____

3. _____big hat_____

4. _____big pants_____

5. _____curly hair_____

Name _____

Teacher Note
Discuss the answers with pupils. Point out that their outlines are short summaries that describe each clown. Ask them for other differences between the two clowns.

23

Read each story. Then write the most important words from the story on the lines below.

1. Shep is a big dog. He stays outside. He chases cars. He barks at the squirrels. Ted plays with Shep.

2. Mitten is a black kitten. She has white feet. She stays in the house. She sleeps in a chair. She drinks milk. She purrs.

1. Shep

   is a big dog

   stays outside

   chases cars

   barks at squirrels

   plays with Ted

2. Mitten

   black kitten

   has white feet

   stays in the house

   sleeps in a chair

   drinks milk

   purrs

Critical Thinking, Level B © 1993 Steck-Vaughn

Name

Teacher Note
Before pupils begin, tell them that summarizing tells a story in a short space. After they have worked independently, discuss their answers. Ask pupils to tell short stories to the class and have other pupils make summaries of these stories.

24

Read each part of the story. Write the answer to each question on the line that comes after it.

The Children's Pets

Tom has a baby duck. It is little and fluffy. It is yellow. The duck says quack.

What is Tom's pet?	I. _____baby duck_____
What size is it?	A. _____little_____
What does it feel like?	B. _____fluffy_____
What color is it?	C. _____yellow_____
What does it say?	D. _____quack_____

Pam has a tiny turtle. Its shell is hard. Its body is soft. It hides its head inside the shell.

What is Pam's pet?	II. _____turtle_____
What size is it?	A. _____tiny_____
What covers it?	B. _____shell_____
What is soft?	C. _____body_____
Where does it hide its head?	D. _____inside shell_____

Name _____

Teacher Note
Tell pupils that an outline is a special type of summarizing. Tell them that they will be making outlines on this page. When they have completed the page independently, discuss their answers.

Read the story. Then fill in the lines on the outline. On each line, tell something about that kind of home.

Indian Homes

The Pueblo Indians lived in homes called **pueblos.** These homes were made of sun-dried earth called **adobe.** The roof of one was the floor of another.

Navajo Indians lived in homes called **hogans.** Hogans were made of logs covered with earth. They had dome-shaped roofs.

Indian Homes

I. Pueblo homes

   A.   made of sun-dried earth called adobe

   B.   roof of one was floor of another

II. Navajo homes

   A.   made of logs covered with earth

   B.   dome-shaped roofs

pueblo

hogan

Name

Critical Thinking, Level B © 1993 Steck-Vaughn

Teacher Note
Read the story about Indian homes to pupils. Work through part I with them. Point out that Roman numerals are used for important things in an outline and that capital letters designate the next most important things. Have pupils complete part II independently.

A. Classifying

Help! The circus wagon broke down! All the animals ran into the pet shop. Circle the animals that belong to the circus. Draw an **X** on the pet shop animals.

B. Definition and Example
Outlining and Summarizing

Finish the outline by writing the names of the animals that go with each definition. Use the **Word Box**.

I. Wild animals used in circuses

    A. _____giraffe_____

    B. _____elephant_____

II. Tame animals used as pets

    A. _____puppy_____

    B. _____kitten_____

Word Box

giraffe

puppy

elephant

kitten

Name _____

Teacher Note
After completing the page, pupils may discuss and check their work with you or a partner.

C. Fact and Opinion
Real and Make-Believe

Read the poems. Write **fact**, **opinion**, or **make-believe**.

A little egg
in a nest of hay.
Cheep-cheep.
Crack-crack.
A little chick
pecked his shell away.
Cheep-cheep.
Crack-crack.

_____
fact

A little white mouse
Playing on a sunbeam
Then sliding back down.

_____
make-believe

I am a nice boy
More than just nice,
Two million times more
The word is ADORABLE.

_____
opinion

Look at the picture.
What do you see?
What can you
imagine? Put your
ideas into a poem.
Write it on a sheet
of paper.

Critical Thinking, Level B © 1993 Steck-Vaughn

Name
_____

Teacher Note
After completing the page, pupils may discuss and check their work with you or a partner.

Understanding

Understanding means telling about something in your own words. Look at the picture. What are the man and the boy doing? What do you think they are talking about? Do you think they know each other? Why or why not?

29

For each row, write the letter of the one that is different.

1.   _D_
   A   B   C   D

2.   _B_
   A   B   C   D

3.   _D_
   A   B   C   D

4.   _C_
   A   B   C   D

5.   _A_
   A   B   C   D

6.   _D_
   A   B   C   D

Name

Critical Thinking, Level B © 1993 Steck-Vaughn

Teacher Note
Before pupils begin, tell them when you compare objects, you look for the ways in which they are alike and different. When you contrast objects, you look for differences. Allow time for pupils to complete the exercise independently.

Read each question. Put a line under the best answer.

1. How are teachers, farmers, and doctors alike?
They all work outdoors.   They are all people.
They all go to school.

2. How are cabins, houses, and tents alike?
They can be moved.   They all have fireplaces.
You can live in them.

3. How are palm trees, apple trees, and grass alike?
They are very tall.   They stay green all winter.
They are plants.

4. How are kittens, calves, and puppies alike?
They are young animals.   They are house pets.
They are the same size.

5. How are trucks, tractors, and cars alike?
They all stay outdoors.   They all have wheels.
They are used only on farms.

6. How are chalk, pencils, and pens alike?
They are used for writing.   They are all sharp.
They all have erasers on them.

7. How are scissors, needles, and thread alike?
They all cut.   They are used for sewing.
They are all used for cooking.

Name _____

Teacher Note
When pupils have completed the page, discuss their answers. Ask them to tell why they did not pick the other choices.

31

On each blank line, write a word from the **Word Box**.

Word Box

birds	beak	little	two	short

Both of these animals are ____birds____ . One bird is

big. The other bird is ____little____ . One bird has long

feathers. The other bird has ____short____ feathers.

Each bird has ____two____ feet and a ____beak____ .

Name

Critical Thinking, Level B © 1993 Steck-Vaughn

Teacher Note
Allow pupils time for independent work. When they have finished, have them make comparisons and contrasts among objects in the classroom.

A. Houses have special parts outside. Look at the parts listed below. Write the number of each part to show where it belongs on the house.

    1. door   4. window

    2. roof   5. steps

    3. brick   6. chimney

B. Houses also have special parts inside. Here is the inside of a house. Write the number of each part on the picture to show where it belongs.

    1. ceiling   4. curtains

    2. floor   5. fireplace

    3. wall   6. bookcase

C. Write a word from the Word Box in each blank.

Word Box

carpet	paint	tile	wallpaper

Cover the inside walls of a house with ____paint____ or

____wallpaper____. Cover the floors with ____carpet____ or

____tile____.

Name _____

Teacher Note
After pupils have completed the page, ask them to identify inside and outside parts of their school. Ask them whether there are any inside parts that can also be found outside, or any outside parts that can be found inside.

Identifying Structure

A. Different words may use the same letters. The order of the letters is different in these words: **tea, ate**. For each Pet Shop Word below, make another word. Use all the letters. The first one is done for you.

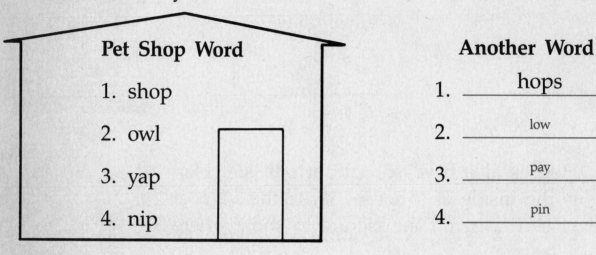

Pet Shop Word	Another Word
1. shop	1. hops
2. owl	2. low
3. yap	3. pay
4. nip	4. pin

B. With some words, you can change one letter to make a new word. Change just one letter in each word on the Dog Word list to make another word that goes with the definition. The first one is done for you.

Dog Word	Definition	New Word
1. puppy	a kind of flower	1. poppy
2. fur	belonging to us	2. our
3. bark	a farm building	3. barn
4. ball	something to ring	4. bell

Name

Critical Thinking, Level B © 1993 Steck-Vaughn

Teacher Note
Guide pupils through the directions in part A. Be sure they understand that only the order is changed in this part. Discuss their answers when they have completed part A. Then have them complete part B independently.

Read the story. Number the pictures in order.

On Saturday morning, Jimmy got up, brushed his teeth, and got dressed. Mother said that breakfast was ready. Jimmy ate breakfast. Then he played outdoors with his sister Alice. When Leon came along, all three children played together.

3 _____

4 _____

1 _____

2 _____

Name _____

Teacher Note
Read the story to pupils, telling them to listen carefully to what happens first, second, third, and fourth in the story. Have them finish the exercise independently.

Read the story. Then number the pictures in order. Use the numbers **1, 2, 3, 4,** and **5.**

Inez decided to make a sock puppet. She used an old sock that she found in her drawer. She cut dog ears out of a piece of brown felt. She glued one ear on each side of the sock. With red and brown markers she drew a dog mouth and nose on the sock. Then she glued on two blue buttons for eyes. When the glue was dry, Inez put her hand in the sock and used her puppet to tell a story.

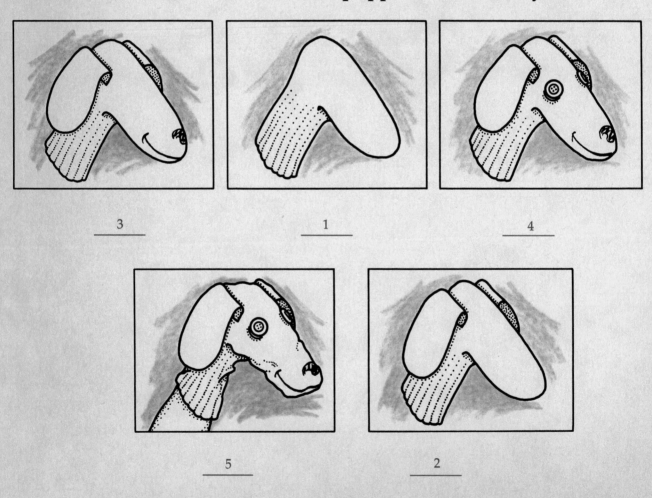

3   1   4

5   2

Name _____

Critical Thinking, Level B © 1993 Steck-Vaughn

Teacher Note
After pupils have completed the page, ask them what Inez might do next with the sock puppet. Pupils might enjoy describing the steps they followed in making something of their own.

36

Write **1**, **2**, and **3** to tell each story in order.

A. __1__ Liz wanted to ride her new bike.

__2__ She rode over to see her friend.

__3__ The two friends rode bikes.

B. __1__ Tom and Jay picked some fruit.

__3__ That night the family ate fruit salad.

__2__ Mother cut up the fruit and made a fruit salad.

C. __3__ Carla began to dance.

__1__ Carla put on her leotards.

__2__ She found her favorite music record.

D. __3__ They bought a western shirt.

__2__ They looked for a shirt for Bob.

__1__ Bob and his father went to the store.

E. __3__ Ann hung the picture in her room.

__2__ She drew a picture of a horse.

__1__ Ann took out her crayons and paper.

Name _____

Teacher Note
Work through part A with pupils. Have them complete the remainder of the exercise independently. Discuss
their answers. Have them tell how they decided which event came first.

Look at the story pictures and read the sentences in the box. Then write the sentences to show what happened first, second, and third.

A. | Tina made a sign and put it up.   Tina built the fort.
Tina got the things to build a fort.

1. ___Tina got the things to build a fort.___

2. ___Tina built the fort.___

3. ___Tina made a sign and put it up.___

B. | The kitten got stuck in a tree.   He rescued the kitten.
Uncle Carlos brought a ladder.

1. ___The kitten got stuck in a tree.___

2. ___Uncle Carlos brought a ladder.___

3. ___He rescued the kitten.___

Name ___

Critical Thinking, Level B © 1993 Steck-Vaughn

Teacher Note
Before pupils begin, have them look at the pictures and tell the stories in their own words. When they have finished, encourage them to tell what might happen next.

Color this shape [g] green.   Color this shape (o) orange.

Color this shape /b\ brown.   Color this [y] and this [y] yellow.

Name

Teacher Note
Have pupils complete this page independently. When checking the exercise, note that the circled letters indicate shapes drawn in perspective. Praise pupils who marked those as indicated as they have exhibited the ability to recognize three-dimensional perspective.

Fourteen letters of the alphabet are hiding here!

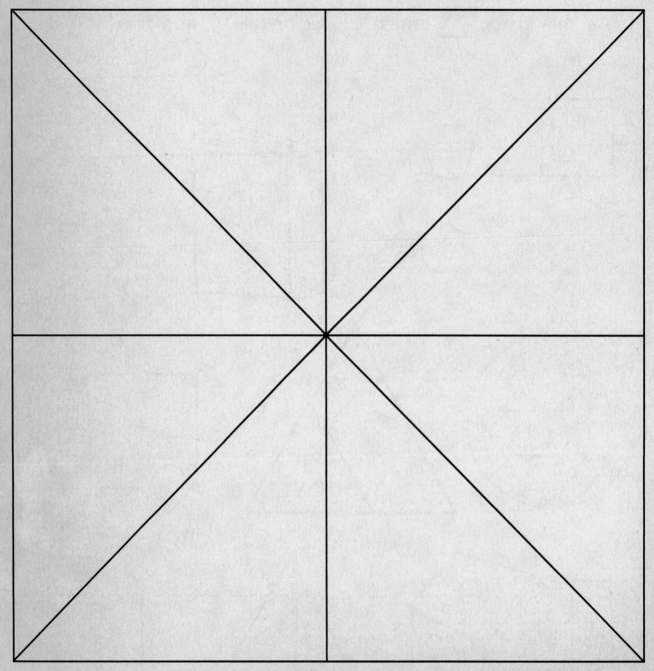

A B C D Ⓔ F G Ⓗ Ⓘ Ⓙ Ⓚ Ⓛ Ⓜ Ⓝ O P Q R S Ⓣ U Ⓥ Ⓦ Ⓧ Ⓨ Ⓩ

Critical Thinking, Level B © 1993 Steck-Vaughn

Name

Teacher Note
Tell pupils that 14 letters with straight lines are hidden on the page. After helping them locate the E and having them trace it with their fingers, have them circle it in the alphabet below. Tell them to complete the exercise in the same way.

40

Write the word that means the same. Then write the word that means the opposite.

	Same	**Opposite**

A. | bad | same | bold | nice | afraid | different |

1. brave   bold   afraid
2. alike   same   different
3. good   nice   bad

B. | dull | mend | big | shining | small | smash |

1. little   small   big
2. bright   shining   dull
3. break   smash   mend

C. | well | fast | tall | slow | short | ill |

1. high   tall   short
2. quick   fast   slow
3. sick   ill   well

Name _____

Teacher Note
Discuss the meanings of the words *same* and *opposite*. Ask for a word that means the same as *cold*—then ask for a word that is its opposite. Work through part A, #1 with pupils. Then allow them time for independent work.

41

Comparing Word Meanings

In each blank, write the correct word from the **Word Box**.

Word Box

be	rode	flour	would	two	wood
to	road	bee	sun	flower	son

Examples: He is the youngest ___son___ of the family.

The ___sun___ is bright today.

1. May we go ___to___ the store?

2. Twins are ___two___ children who often look alike.

3. Jane ___rode___ the horse for a long time.

4. The car was on the ___road___.

5. A tulip is a kind of ___flower___.

6. I use ___flour___ when I bake.

7. Lee wants to ___be___ a teacher.

8. The ___bee___ stung me on the arm.

9. We ___would___ like to go with you.

10. The chair is made of ___wood___.

FINEST FLOUR

Critical Thinking, Level B © 1993 Steck-Vaughn

Name _____

Teacher Note
Tell pupils that some words sound the same but have different meanings. Help them pronounce the words in the Word Box. Discuss the example. After they have completed the lesson independently, go over their answers with them.

Circle the best title for each story.

A.   Spot is a little gray pony. He lives on a farm. One day, Mei was riding Spot. Spot stepped into a hole. He hurt his leg. The doctor had to fix it.

> 1. (Spot's Hurt Leg)
> 2. Mei Loves Spot
> 3. A Little Gray Pony

B.   The turtle and the hippo had a race. The hippo went faster than the turtle. It finished the race before the turtle did. The turtle said, "I enjoyed our race."

> 1. Angry Turtle
> 2. (The Speedy Hippo)
> 3. The Elephant's Friends

C.   People keep many kinds of pets in their homes. Some have dogs or cats. Others have birds or fish. Some people even have tame monkeys!

> 1. Sally's Pets
> 2. People Need Pets
> 3. (Kinds of House Pets)

Name
_____

Teacher Note
Tell pupils that the best title is one which contains the main idea of the story. Read the first story to them and help them find the best title. When they have finished the page, have pupils tell short stories and have other pupils suggest titles.

Read each story. Then underline the sentence in the box that tells the main idea.

1.   A cactus is a spiny plant. It grows in the desert. It needs very little water.

| It is hot in the desert. |
| Cactus is a desert plant. |

2.   Oranges grow on trees. First they are green. Then they turn yellow. At last they turn orange.

| Oranges change color. |
| Oranges are juicy. |

3.   The part of a carrot that you eat is the root. It grows under the ground. It has lacy green leaves on top.

| Carrots taste good. |
| Carrots are root vegetables. |

4.   Cotton grows in places where it is hot. It needs lots of sunshine and water. When the cotton pods get very big, they burst open.

| Some clothes are made of cotton. |
| Cotton needs warm weather. |

Name

Critical Thinking, Level B © 1993 Steck-Vaughn

Teacher Note
Have pupils complete the exercise independently. Discuss their answers with them. Ask pupils why they did not choose the other sentences.

Read each story. Circle the sentence that tells the main idea.

1.   Jackie tied on her bonnet. Then she laced up her high-top shoes. (Jackie was getting ready for a costume party.)

2.   (The parade was so much fun!) We saw floats and banners. There were clowns and bands. There were even dancing dogs.

3.   First you see streaks of light. Then the sky gets lighter and lighter. (A sunrise is very beautiful.)

4.   (Mark wanted to paint a picture.) He set up his easel and paints. He found paper and brushes. Then he spread paper on the floor.

Name _____

Teacher Note
After pupils have finished the page, ask them to tell why they underlined the sentences they did. Have them tell what clues they used.

Circle the word that tells what the story is about. Then draw a line under the main idea sentence.

Example: (Kites) are lots of fun. You have to run fast to get them flying. Then the kites dance in the air.

1. Here is how to make a (mask). Get a big paper bag. Then use scissors to cut eyeholes. Use paint and yarn to finish the funny face.

2. (Skyrockets) are beautiful. Their colors flash in the night sky. People enjoy watching the colors pop and drop through the dark.

3. (Tadpoles) are young frogs. At first they look more like fish than frogs. They wiggle through the water. Soon they grow legs and can hop on the ground.

4. Ben got a (surprise) for his birthday. The surprise was gray and white. The surprise said, "Meow." Ben gave the surprise a bowl of milk.

5. Nancy filled the washtub with water. Next she found Bowser's soap and tub toy. Nancy was going to give her dog a (bath).

6. The sun gives us light. It makes the air warm. It helps things grow. The (sun) is important to everything on Earth.

Name

Critical Thinking, Level B © 1993 Steck-Vaughn

Teacher Note
Before pupils begin, work through the example with them. Then allow time for individual work. Discuss the correct answers.

Identifying Relationships

Write a number to show where each person is going.

Name

Teacher Note
After pupils have completed the work independently, ask them how they decided where each person was going. Ask what clues the pictures gave them. List some other places to go—the store, a movie, the playground—and ask what they would take to these places.

Identifying Relationships

Read each job name in the middle. Draw lines to show two things used by a person who does that job.

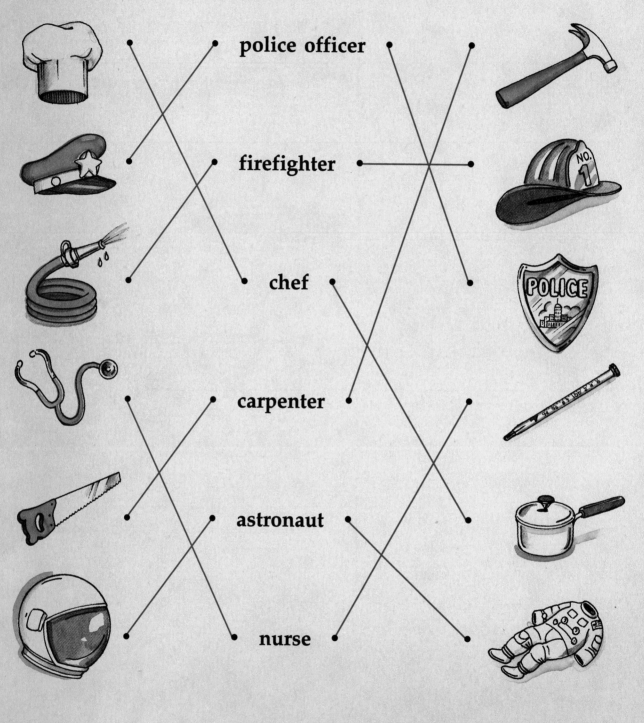

police officer

firefighter

chef

carpenter

astronaut

nurse

Name _____

Critical Thinking, Level B © 1993 Steck-Vaughn

Teacher Note
After pupils complete the page, ask them to name other things that might belong to these people and to tell what they are used for. Name other jobs—farmer, paramedic, baseball player, musician—and ask pupils to name items that might belong to someone who does each job.

Write the letter of the picture that will fill each blank correctly.

A   B   C   D

E   F   G   H

1. It is raining, so you will need an __C__ if you go out.

2. If you want to color, you will need __B__.

3. If you drop the __D__, it will break.

4. Some people like to read, so they need __A__.

5. If the __E__ shines, the __F__ will melt.

6. To catch a __G__, you need a __H__.

Name _____

Teacher Note
Before pupils work on this lesson, be sure they can name the things shown in each picture. When they have finished, ask them to make up other sentences similar to those on this page. You may need to get them started—for example, *If you have a toothache, you should* _____.

Identifying Relationships

Read each sentence. Fill in each blank with the correct word from the **Word Box**.

Word Box

Tuesday	bat	pencil	nail	hungry	water
baseball	won	apple	out	party	red

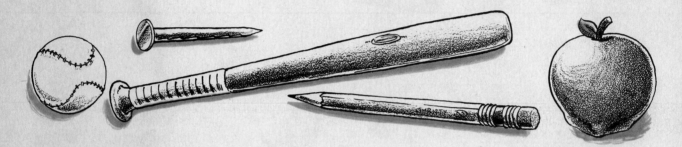

1. Eva ran faster than Sam, so Eva ____won____ the race.

2. Ben stepped on a rusty ____nail____, so he went to the doctor.

3. Since the sun is ____out____, we can go on a picnic.

4. Tina wanted to write, so she got a ____pencil____.

5. It was John's birthday, so we gave him a ____party____.

6. Yesterday was Monday, so today must be ____Tuesday____.

7. Lucy lost her green socks, so she wore her ____red____ ones.

8. If you are thirsty, drink some ____water____.

9. To play ____baseball____, you need a ____bat____.

10. Paul was ____hungry____, so he ate an ____apple____.

Name _____

Critical Thinking, Level B © 1993 Steck-Vaughn

Teacher Note
Read the words in the Word Box to pupils. Allow them individual time to work on the exercise. Give examples for pupils to complete orally after they have finished.

50

A. Identifying Relationships
Understanding Pictures

Draw a line from each sentence to the thing the animal needs.

The deer is thirsty.

The bird wants to build a nest.

The bee wants to fly home.

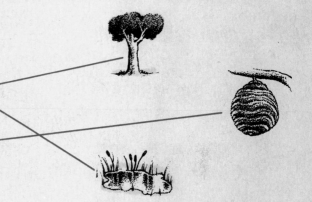

B. Steps in a Process
Identifying Main Ideas

The directions for building a doghouse are below, but they are all mixed up. Write **1** before the step that comes first, **2** before the second step, and so on.

___3___ Build the roof.

___1___ Get wood, hammers, and nails.

___4___ Paint the doghouse.

___2___ Build the sides of the house.

On the line below, write a title for your directions.

How to Build a Doghouse
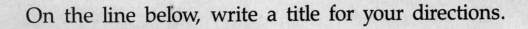

Name

Teacher Note
After completing the page pupils may discuss and check their work with you or a partner.

51

C. Identifying Structure

An animal name is hiding in each of the words below. Circle the letters that name the animal. The first one is done for you.

1. b(o x)   3. c(a p e)   5. s(p i g)o t

2. c(r a t)e   4. h(e e l)   6. l(a n(t)e r n)

D. Comparing and Contrasting
Comparing Word Meanings

You can write some words so that they **look** like what they mean.

FAT   thin   **TALL**   **SHORT**

In the space below, write the following word pairs so they look like what they mean.

beautiful ugly   happy sad   straight bent

Name
_____

Critical Thinking, Level B © 1993 Steck-Vaughn

Teacher Note
After completing the page, pupils may discuss and check their work with you or a partner.

52

Applying

Teacher Note
In order to develop Bloom's third stage—applying—the pupil needs to engage in the following skills:
• Ordering Objects
• Estimating
• Thinking About What Will Happen
• Inferring
• Interpreting Changes in Word Meanings

Applying means using what you know. Let's try it out. Look at the picture. Did someone in the picture say something funny? How do you know? Do you think one of the girls told the joke? Why or why not?

53

Ordering Objects

Put the pictures in each row in order. The first picture has **1** under it. Write **2**, **3**, and **4** on the correct lines.

A.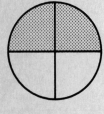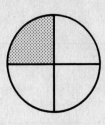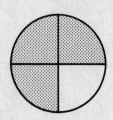

       3   2   4   1

B.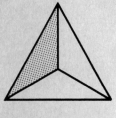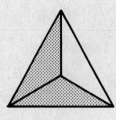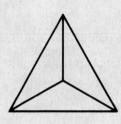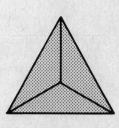

       2   3   1   4

C.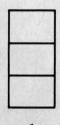

       2   1   4   3

D.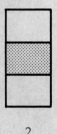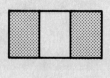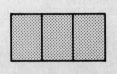

       2   3   1   4

Name

Critical Thinking, Level B © *1993 Steck-Vaughn*

Teacher Note
Before pupils begin, do part A with them. Be sure they understand that the progression in the figures is from no shading to most shading. When they have finished, have them draw a similar progression with four identical shapes.

For each row decide what comes next. Draw it.

1.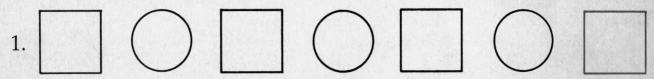

2.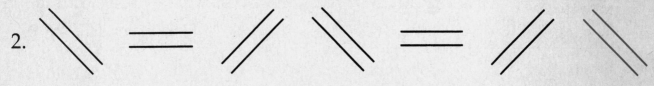

3.

4. L M N O P Q R S

5.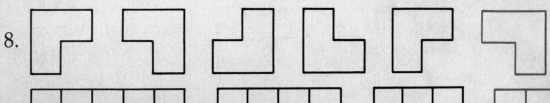

6. PxA PxB PxC PxD PxE

7. 19 17 15 13 11 9 7

8.

9.

Name _____

Teacher Note
Be sure pupils understand the directions before they begin. Discuss how they should complete #1 and then have them complete the exercise independently.

For each row, draw step 3.

A.

Drawing should
show three
balloons.

1.   2.   3.   4.

B.

Drawing should
show two birds
hatched, one egg
still unhatched.

1.   2.   3.   4.

C.

Drawing should show
one mitten and one
boot *or* two boots.

1.   2.   3.   4.

Critical Thinking, Level B © 1993 Steck-Vaughn.

Name

Teacher Note
Discuss part A with pupils, making sure they understand the directions. Allow them individual time to
complete the exercise.

Will the things pictured on the right fit into the container?
If so, mark **X** on the line.

_____

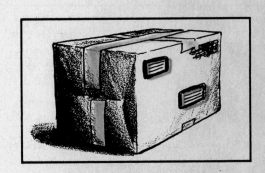

_____

 X

 X

Name

Teacher Note
Tell pupils that estimating has to do with forming a general idea of the size, value, or cost of something. When they have finished the page, have pupils discuss their answers. Ask them what would fit in the small container and the mailbox.

Estimating

Circle the picture that answers each question.

1. Which ball will fit in the box?

2. Which mitten will fit best?

3. Which drapes will fit best on the window?

4. Which tie will fit best on the shirt?

5. Which saucer will fit best with the cup?

6. Which collar will fit best on the dog?

7. Which box will fit on the shelf?

Name _____

Teacher Note
Make sure pupils can identify the pictures in the left-hand column before they begin. Tell them they are to estimate which object will fit each of these. Then have pupils complete the page independently.

Estimating

Study the map. Then answer the questions.

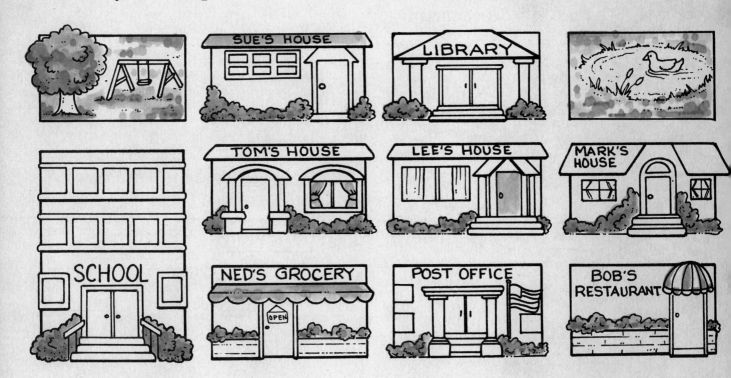

1. Whose house is closest to the store?

   Tom's house
   _____

2. Whose house is farthest from the school?

   Mark's house
   _____

3. Which is closer to the school—the pond or the park?

   the park
   _____

4. Whose house is farthest from the restaurant?

   Sue's house
   _____

5. Who lives across the street from the post office and the library?

   Lee
   _____

Name

_____

Teacher Note
Before pupils begin, read the names of the places to them. After discussing their answers, ask pupils to
estimate the number of steps to different parts of the classroom and then have individuals actually walk each
distance.

Circle the answer in each box that tells how long it would probably take to do each thing.

1. (30 seconds) 30 minutes

2. (30 minutes) 8 hours

3. (2 years) 7 days

4. 3 seconds (2 minutes)

5. (15 minutes) 6 hours

6. 10 seconds (4 minutes)

Critical Thinking, Level B © 1993 Steck-Vaughn

Name _____

Teacher Note
Before pupils begin the page, you may wish to review the time concepts of second, minute, hour, day, and year. Make sure pupils know what action is taking place in each picture before they begin work. When they have finished, ask them to explain their answer choices.

Look at each set of pictures. Then read the three sentences.
Put an **X** before the sentence that tells what will happen next.

A.

_____ 1. The dog will take a nap.

__X__ 2. The dog will run away.

_____ 3. The dog will eat its food.

B.

__X__ 1. Jean will take a picture.

_____ 2. Jean will ask someone to
take a picture.

_____ 3. Jean has a camera that
does not work.

C.

_____ 1. Hugo will play a game.

_____ 2. Hugo will color a picture.

__X__ 3. Hugo will write a story.

D.

_____ 1. Her family will eat the
plant.

__X__ 2. Her family will enjoy the
flowers.

_____ 3. Sue will throw the flowers
away.

Name

Teacher Note
After pupils complete the page, ask them what else might happen. For example, might the dog in part A stay
near the stake instead of running away? Might his owner catch him before he is able to run away?

Read the beginning of each sentence. Circle the correct sentence ending.

1. If you plant a seed, it should

     die.   get smaller.   (grow.)   blow away.

2. When you write a word, you want others to

     (read it.)   cross it out.   erase it.   lose it.

3. When you go to a party, you want to

     be sad.   get sick.   go home.   (have fun.)

4. If you pack a suitcase, you are ready to

     (go on a trip.)   go to school.   eat.   get lost.

5. Pretend the temperature is zero. You will be

     hot.   warm.   (cold.)   cool.

6. If you lose some money, you will be

     (sad.)   glad.   happy.   tired.

7. When your team wins, you feel

     (good.)   bad.   silly.   sorry.

8. If you get a letter from a friend, you will

     lose it.   drop it.   find it.   (read it.)

Name _____

Critical Thinking, Level B © 1993 Steck-Vaughn

Teacher Note
Discuss with pupils the fact that when you think about what might happen, you may think of several outcomes but that there is usually one that is *most* likely. In #1, for example, the seed might die or blow away if you don't plant it properly, but it is most likely it will grow.

Read each sentence beginning. Finish the sentence in your own way.

1. If rabbits moved into my house, I would _____ Sentences will vary.

   _____ .

2. If a dog ate my boots, I would _____

   _____ .

3. If a space creature came to my house, I would _____

   _____ .

4. If I could ride in the space shuttle, I would _____

   _____ .

5. If it snowed on the Fourth of July, I would _____

   _____ .

Name _____

Teacher Note
Have pupils read their answers aloud when they have finished. Emphasize the variety of possible outcomes.
Ask pupils whether they consider all the answers acceptable.

Put on your thinking cap! Ready? OK. Write sentences to answer these questions.

1. Do you think life on the earth would change if it stayed light 24 hours a day? How?

   Responses will vary.
   _____
   _____
   _____

2. If it never rained again, would it change the way we live? How?

   _____
   _____
   _____

3. How would our lives change if we no longer had cars or buses or trains or planes?

   _____
   _____
   _____

Name _____

Teacher Note
After pupils have finished the exercise, have them read their answers aloud. Encourage expression of disagreements and toleration of classmates' viewpoints.

Inferring

Write **yes** if you are sure that the sentence is true. Write **no** if you cannot be sure that the sentence is true.

1.

This ring could
belong only to Jane. _____no_____

2.

Mary lives in this
apartment house. _____no_____

3.

It is winter. _____yes_____

4.

The black horse
will win. _____no_____

5.

Meili caught
this fish. _____no_____

6.

The boy is riding
the bicycle. _____yes_____

Name
_____

Teacher Note
Explain to pupils that *inferring* involves drawing conclusions from facts or ideas. Go over the directions, making sure pupils understand they are to put *yes* only if they are sure the answer is true. If they have any doubts, they must answer *no*.

Read each story. Circle the picture that answers the question at the end of the story. Then put an **X** before the sentence that tells why you chose that picture.

A. John was watching a TV show. A man was crossing the desert. John could almost feel the hot sun. Soon, John ran to get something he wanted very much. What do you think it was?

What makes you think so?

1. _____ When you cross a desert, you need something to ride on.

2. __X__ John was thirsty. He felt as if he were trying to cross the desert, too.

3. _____ John was tired of watching TV and wanted to play.

B. Mother needed to go shopping. She had a list and her purse. Mother got into the car. She could not start it. She asked Lupe to get something for her. What did Mother want Lupe to get?

What makes you think so?

1. _____ Mother wanted to buy toys.

2. _____ The box can carry the groceries.

3. __X__ You need a key to start a car.

Name _____

Critical Thinking, Level B © 1993 Steck-Vaughn

Teacher Note
Make sure pupils understand the directions before they begin. After they have completed the page independently, discuss the answers.

Read each story. Then follow the directions.

A.   A woman left some letters at Dot's house. One was from Dot's uncle. Circle the name of the person who left the letters.

> Dot's uncle
>
> (the mail carrier)
>
> Dot

Put an **X** in front of the reason for your choice.

1. _____ Dot lives there.

2. _____ Dot's uncle wrote the letter.

3. __X__ The mail carrier delivers mail to houses.

B.   Jack said, "What am I thinking of? The animal has little front legs, long back legs, and a pocket. It hops around on its back legs." Circle the name of the animal Jack is thinking of.

> a rabbit
>
> a monkey
>
> (a kangaroo)

Put an **X** in front of the reason for your choice.

1. _____ Monkeys have four long legs for swinging.

2. _____ Rabbits have strong back legs and long ears.

3. __X__ Kangaroos have strong back legs and a pocket.

Name

Teacher Note
Go over the directions with pupils before they begin the exercise. When they have completed the page, ask them to tell why they did not choose the other reasons.

Read each story. In the blank, write the correct word from the story.

1. Carlos was walking down the street. He saw something fall from a girl's purse. He found a dime on the sidewalk.

   A _____ dime _____ fell from the purse.

2. Father told Sue to finish her work after dinner. Sue finished dinner. Now she has to finish her _____ work _____.

3. Tomatoes must be picked as soon as they ripen. The tomatoes are ripe now. They must be _____ picked _____.

4. On Wednesday the school lunchroom serves pizza. Today is Wednesday. The children will have _____ pizza _____ for lunch.

5. Frank must shovel snow before he plays. He has shoveled the snow. Now Frank can _____ play _____.

Name _____

Teacher Note
Before pupils begin, tell them that they are to infer the correct answer from the story and that no other information is necessary. When they have finished the page, go over their answers with them.

Read each sentence. Think about how the word **run** is used. Find that meaning in the box. Write its number on the line after the sentence.

A.

The stream runs under the bridge. ___1___

B.

Our house is on her run. ___4___

C.

Windmills can run. ___5___

D.

They can run an errand. ___3___

E.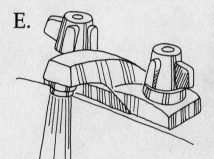

The faucet runs. ___2___

F.

The boy runs. ___6___

Meanings

1. goes from one place to another
2. the water comes out
3. do something for someone
4. usual trip
5. go around
6. goes fast

Name

Teacher Note
Explain to pupils that the same words can be used in many different ways. Tell them that the word *run* is used in six different ways on this page. After discussion of the correct answers, have pupils volunteer words—for example, *guard*, *hand*—with multiple meanings.

69

Read the words and their meanings. Then read each sentence. Put the letter of the correct meaning for each underlined word in front of each sentence.

Word Meanings

fly
  A. insect with wings
  B. move through the air with wings

roll
  A. kind of bread
  B. turn over and over

ring
  A. give out a sound
  B. thin circle of metal

___A___ The fly landed on the flower.

___B___ Birds fly south in the winter.

___B___ Dad gave me a ring for my birthday.

___A___ Did the phone ring?

___A___ Maria wants a roll with her dinner.

___B___ Let's roll down the hill.

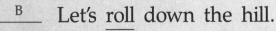

Name _____

Critical Thinking, Level B © 1993 Steck-Vaughn

Teacher Note
Discuss their answers when pupils have completed the exercise. Other words you might want to discuss with them are *cold*, *pen*, and *cut*.

70

Read each sentence. Find a word in the **Word Box** that has the same meaning as the underlined words. Write the word on the line.

Word Box

left	give	finished	help	come	watch	borrowed

1. Mike <u>took out</u> a book. _borrowed_

2. Tina will <u>lend a hand</u>. _help_

3. <u>Hand over</u> the jump rope to Jan. _give_

4. Please <u>keep an eye on</u> the baby. _watch_

5. The airplane <u>took off</u>. _left_

6. The game is <u>all over</u>. _finished_

7. Night has <u>fallen</u>. _come_

Name _____

Teacher Note
Tell pupils that this page is primarily concerned with *idioms*, expressions that cannot be understood from the meanings of their separate words but must be learned as a whole. Have pupils complete the page independently. Then ask them to tell what each of the underlined items means literally.

Write a word from the box to finish each sentence. When you finish the story, go back and circle the correct meaning of each word.

bill	(A. bird's beak)	B. list of what is owed
pet	(A. stroke or pat)	B. animal kept by a person
left	A. opposite of right	(B. went away from)
pen	A. something for writing	(B. fenced place for animals)
line	A. long, thin mark	(B. straight row)

Miss Cody's class was excited. They were going to visit the children's zoo. They stood in a long _____line_____ with other people at the gate. Once inside, they saw all kinds of animals. They went into a wooden _____pen_____ where there were friendly sheep. They admired the big bright _____bill_____ of a toucan in a huge bird cage. They even got to gently _____pet_____ a baby rabbit. They were very tired when they finally _____left_____ the zoo at the day's end.

Critical Thinking, Level B © 1993 Steck-Vaughn

Name _____

Teacher Note
Before pupils begin, review the directions. Then read the story with them, pausing at each blank. When pupils have completed the page, discuss their answers.

A. Ordering Objects
   Estimating
   Inferring

1. The boat race is about to start! First, the boats must line up according to size. Write **1** on the smallest boat, **2** on the next smallest, and so on up to **6**.

2. Look at **Zip** and **Princess**. Which one uses the most gas?

   Princess

   Tell why you think so. ___It is larger than Zip.___

3. Look at **Flipper** and **Plug**. Which one can go faster if just one

   person is in it? ___Flipper___

   Tell why you think so. ___It is lighter. (or) It is made for just one person.___

Name

Teacher Note
After completing the page, pupils may discuss and check their work with you or a partner.

B. Thinking About What Will Happen

Read the first two parts of the poem. Then finish the poem using the lines in the **Rhyme Line Box**.

One, **one**
Cinnamon **bun**

Two, **two**
Chicken **stew**

Three, three

Cakes and tea
_____

Four, four

I want more
_____

Rhyme Line Box

I want more

Cakes and tea

C. Changes in Word Meanings

It's fun to make up new words. Look at the new word one writer made up. Then make up your own new words to go in the sentences.

A **thrickle** is a tickle in the back of your throat.

1. The place where lost socks go is a ___Answers will vary.___ .

2. The button on top of a baseball cap is a _____ .

Name

Critical Thinking, Level B © 1993 Steck-Vaughn

Teacher Note
After completing the page, pupils may discuss their work with you or a partner.

Analyzing

Teacher Note

In order to develop Bloom's fourth stage—analyzing—the pupil needs to engage in the following skills:
- Judging Completeness
- Thinking About Facts That Fit
- Distinguishing Abstract from Concrete
- Judging Logic of Actions
- Identifying Parts of a Story
- Examining Story Logic
- Recognizing True and False

Analyzing means seeing how parts fit together. What do you see in this picture? What is the girl doing? Why do you think she is drinking the water? Where is the water coming from? How do you know?

Judging Completeness

Finish drawing each picture.

Name

Critical Thinking, Level B © 1993 Steck-Vaughn

Teacher Note
Tell pupils to finish this exercise independently. Then have them come to the blackboard in pairs. Have one
pupil draw the beginning of an object and have the other complete it.

Judging Completeness

Read each sentence. Study the picture. Complete the sentence with a word from the **Word Box**.

Word Box

hands	wheel	door	picture	handle	short

1. The frame has no

   <u>   picture   </u>.

2. The wagon needs a

   <u>   wheel   </u>.

3. One leg is too

   <u>   short   </u>.

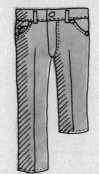

4. The pitcher needs a

   <u>   handle   </u>.

5. The house has no

   <u>   door   </u>.

6. The clock has no

   <u>   hands   </u>.

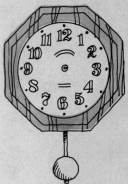

Name _____

Teacher Note
Make sure pupils understand the directions before having them complete the page independently. After discussing the correct answers, have pupils volunteer sentences lacking last words. Have other pupils finish these sentences.

A word is missing from each sentence below. Add a word from the box to complete each sentence and to tell about the picture. Write the new sentence.

magician	acrobats	bicycle	rings	wire

1. A little clown rode a huge.

   A little clown rode a huge bicycle.

2. Three strong made a pyramid.

   Three strong acrobats made a pyramid.

3. A pulled an umbrella from a top hat.

   A magician pulled an umbrella from a top hat.

4. A woman walked on a up in the air.

   A woman walked on a wire in the air.

5. A juggler threw high into the air.

   A juggler threw rings high into the air.

Name

Critical Thinking, Level B © 1993 Steck-Vaughn

Teacher Note
Read the page directions with pupils. Make sure they understand that each sentence is missing a word. Explain that they are to complete and rewrite each sentence using picture clues.

For each part, put an **X** before the two things you feel are most important.

1. You are going to a friend's birthday party. You need to know

   __X__ where the party will be.

   __X__ what time the party will be.

   _____ how many people will be there.

2. You are going to the circus. You need to know

   __X__ how to get there.

   _____ why a circus has animals.

   __X__ how much it will cost.

3. You want to make a garden. You should know

   _____ how many of your friends eat vegetables.

   __X__ how to plant a seed.

   __X__ how often to water the garden.

4. Your friend will make a valentine. He will need

   __X__ paste and scissors.

   __X__ some kind of paper.

   _____ a book telling about holidays.

Name _____

Teacher Note
After pupils have completed the page, discuss their answers with them. Ask them why the phrases they marked are important to each activity. Ask them, in addition, why they did not mark the other phrases.

A. Read the story.

    Carol was going on a trip with her family. Who would take care of her little brown hamster while she was gone?

    "I'll be glad to do that for you," said Carol's friend Lee.

    Carol took her hamster to Lee's house. "This hamster's name is Wheelo," said Carol. "That's because his favorite toy is this wheel he runs around on. The main thing is to keep Wheelo healthy. He needs food three times a day. He needs water all the time. He has to be in a warm place."

    "What's this little cage for?" asked Lee.

    "You have to clean Wheelo's cage twice a week," said Carol. "Put him in the little cage while you clean his big one."

B. Put an **X** before the four most important rules.

Taking Care of a Hamster

1. __X__ Feed it on time.

2. _____ Know the hamster's name.

3. __X__ Keep the hamster warm.

4. _____ Give the hamster a wheel.

5. _____ Know the color of the hamster.

6. __X__ Make sure the hamster has water.

7. _____ Play with the hamster.

8. __X__ Clean the cage.

Name _____

Critical Thinking, Level B © 1993 Steck-Vaughn

Teacher Note
Read the story about Wheelo to pupils. When they have completed the exercise, discuss their answers. Have pupils explain why 2, 4, 5, and 7 are not as important.

Lisa is going to have a birthday party. Let's wrap some presents for her. Which things in the list below could you wrap and give to Lisa? Put an **X** before each one.

X a ring	X a toy car	____ a dream
____ fog	____ a good idea	X a doll
____ a nice time	X a purse	X an umbrella
X a skirt	____ a little better	X a puzzle
____ a smile	____ noise	X a hat
X a baseball	X a game	X a watch
____ a sunny day	____ a week	____ a lot of help

Name _____

Teacher Note
Define the terms *abstract* and *concrete* for pupils. Concrete things can be touched or felt, but abstract things can only be thought about. Ask pupils to name some concrete objects in the classroom. Then have them give abstract words to these objects. Allow individual time for completion of the page.

81

Abstract or Concrete

Study the **Word Box**. On the lines in part 1, write words that name things you can only **think** about. In part 2, write words that name things you can **touch**.

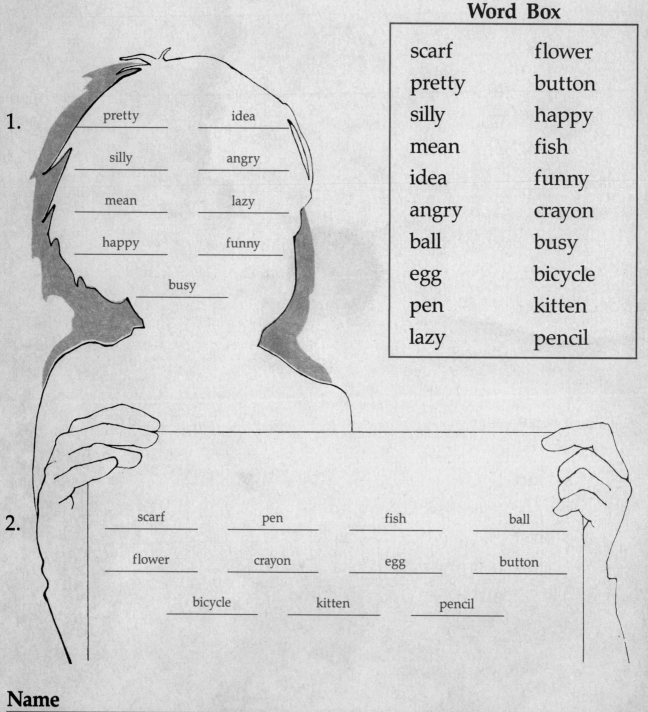

Word Box

scarf	flower
pretty	button
silly	happy
mean	fish
idea	funny
angry	crayon
ball	busy
egg	bicycle
pen	kitten
lazy	pencil

1.
pretty   idea

silly   angry

mean   lazy

happy   funny

busy

2.
scarf   pen   fish   ball

flower   crayon   egg   button

bicycle   kitten   pencil

Name

Critical Thinking, Level B © 1993 Steck-Vaughn

Teacher Note
Make sure pupils understand the directions before letting them work on this page independently. After discussing the correct answers, ask pupils to think of more examples in each group.

A. Look at the square at the right. Read about what it shows.

Joe's tennis shoe is part of a larger group of all tennis shoes. Tennis shoes are part of a larger group of all shoes. Shoes are part of a still larger group of all clothes.

B. Write these words in the squares where they belong.

| furniture | my rocking chair | oak trees |

Name _____

Teacher Note
Guide pupils through the reading of the explanation at the top of the page, referring them to the accompanying illustration. Then direct their attention to the two squares at the bottom of the page. Work as a group to determine where the words in the box should go.

83

Read the words in the squares and the **Word List**. Write words from the **Word List** on the correct lines inside the squares.

Word List

1. people
2. toys with wheels
3. cherry tomatoes
4. tomatoes
5. my parents
6. fruits and vegetables

A.

all toys

toys with wheels
_____

all
skates

my
skates

B.

people
_____

my family

my parents
_____

Dad

C.

foods

fruits and vegetables
_____

tomatoes
_____

cherry

tomatoes
_____

Name

_____

Critical Thinking, Level B © 1993 Steck-Vaughn

Teacher Note
You may wish to review page 83 with pupils. Read the words in the Word List to them. Work on part A together. Have pupils complete the page independently.

A. Read each question. Find the answer in the Word Box. Write the word on the line.

kneel	run	jump	climb	sit

_____sit_____ 1. What do you do when you eat dinner?

_____run_____ 2. What do you do if you want to go faster?

_____kneel_____ 3. What must you do to paint the bottom of a door?

_____climb_____ 4. What do you do to go up?

_____jump_____ 5. What can you do with a rope?

B. Circle each thing someone might take on a camping trip.

Name

_____

Teacher Note
After pupils complete the page, discuss their answers. Have them explain why it makes no sense to take a couch, mailbox, or piano on a camping trip. Ask them to name other items they might take on a camping trip.

Look at the pictures and words under them. Read each sentence. If the boy could use **all three things** to do that job, draw a line under the sentence.

scissors   paint   glue

1. He could help fix a bulletin board.

2. He could fix breakfast.

3. He could decorate his toy box.

4. He could make a picture.

5. He could mow the grass.

6. He could make a get-well card.

7. He could make a storybook.

8. He could fix his wagon.

Name

Critical Thinking, Level B © 1993 Steck-Vaughn

Teacher Note
Read the directions to the pupils. Be sure they understand that they underline a sentence only if the boy could use *all* three things. After discussing the answers, have pupils tell what things they could use to fix breakfast, repair a wagon, or mow grass.

Logic of Actions

A. Read the list of people's jobs in the box. Write the name of the person who would best solve each problem.

dentist	veterinarian	police officer
plumber	mechanic	doctor

1. You would call a ___plumber___ if you had a leaky sink.

2. You would call a ___police officer___ if you saw a lost child.

3. You would call a ___veterinarian___ if your dog was sick.

4. You would call a ___doctor___ if you weren't feeling well.

5. You would call a ___mechanic___ if your car wouldn't start.

6. You would call a ___dentist___ if you had a tooth that hurt.

B. Finish each sentence by putting an **X** in front of the part that makes sense.

1. Mom's birthday is coming, so Peter should buy a _____ .

   __X__ present for her   _____ book for himself

2. Maria's best friend is sick so she should _____ .

   __X__ send a get well card   _____ invite her over this afternoon

3. Andres is leaving on a trip tomorrow so he should _____ .

   _____ go roller skating   __X__ start packing a suitcase

Name

Teacher Note
Before pupils begin work, read aloud the list of occupations in the box. Discuss what the job of each person generally includes. Then have pupils complete the page independently.

Find the word in each sentence that does **not** make sense. Circle it. Find a word in the **Word Box** that **would** make sense. Write it on the line.

_____flew_____ 1. Rita and Rudy (ran) to Mexico in a huge airplane.

_____airport_____ 2. Grandfather met them at the (station).

_____Mexico_____ 3. Rita and Rudy visited a school while they were in (Spain).

_____friends_____ 4. They made many new (enemies) in Mexico.

_____hotel_____ 5. Rita and Rudy slept in a big (school).

_____airplane_____ 6. They got on the same (train) to go home.

_____trip_____ 7. They told friends at home about their (circus).

_____train_____ 8. The next year they rode a (camel) to Canada.

_____rode_____ 9. Rita and Rudy (walked) home in a car.

Word Box

friends
airplane
flew
hotel
trip
rode
airport
train
Mexico

Critical Thinking, Level B © 1993 Steck-Vaughn

Name _____

Teacher Note
Tell pupils that all the sentences on this page tell a story about two children who went to Mexico. Read the directions and the Word Box words to pupils. Work #1 as a group before pupils finish the exercise independently.

88

Parts of a Story

A. A story has characters. WHO?
   A story has a setting. WHERE?
   Read the story. Then follow your teacher's directions.

The (robot) was standing in the toy store window. It didn't
like it there. It wanted someone to take it home and play
with it.
   Rosa walked by the store with her grandpa.
   "Oh, what a wonderful robot!" said Rosa.
   "I will get it for you for your birthday," said Grandpa.
   Grandpa and Rosa went into the store. Grandpa bought the
robot. He and Rosa drove it home in the car. The robot
enjoyed the ride.
   Rosa played with the robot. Now the robot was happy, and
so was Rosa!

B. A story has action. WHAT HAPPENED?
   Complete each sentence with a word from the story.

   1. Rosa wanted the __robot_____.

   2. Rosa and Grandpa went into the __store_____.

   3. They took the new toy home in Grandpa's __car_____.

   4. Rosa played with the __robot_____.

   5. Rosa felt __happy_____.

Name _____

Teacher Note
After pupils read the story independently, tell them to circle the word that tells the first character in the story.
Tell them to put X's on the names of the two people in the story. Tell them to draw a line under the words
that tell where the robot was when the story began.

89

Read the story. Then follow your teacher's directions.

The school bus stopped at the corner. The bus ~~driver~~ looked around. Then the bus went on.

~~Brian~~ saw the bus. Brian was running along the sidewalk. But he was not at the corner in time. Poor Brian! (He missed the bus!)

Brian stood on the corner. He had tears in his eyes. What should he do?

Then his ~~mother~~ came along in her car.

"What is wrong, Brian?" she asked.

"I missed the bus," Brian answered.

✓ "Hop in. I'll take you to school." she said.

Name

Teacher Note
Tell pupils to: 1) put an X on the names of the people in the story; 2) draw a line under the two sentences that tell where Brian was; 3) circle the sentence that tells what happened to Brian when he didn't get to the corner in time; and 4) put a check by the sentence that tells what Mom will do.

A. Use the numbers 1-5 to show the story in order.
   Write the numbers on the lines under the pictures.

3

4 or 5

1

4 or 5

2

B. What three things might the clown do after the show?
   Tell the things in order.

1. _Answers will vary._

2. _____

3. _____

Name _____

Teacher Note
After pupils have finished the page independently, ask them to read what they have written in the blanks.
Accept all logical answers and solicit the class's opinions about the answers that are not ordered correctly.

Read the words in the **Word Box**. Then read the story. Write a word from the **Word Box** in each blank.

Word Box

path	noise	Jeff	glad
leaves	dark	walking	run
dog	feet	Rags	afraid

One day Jeff went ___walking___ in the woods.

As he walked, he heard the dry ___leaves___ under his

___feet___. He saw many tall trees. It was ___dark___

in the woods. Then ___Jeff___ saw some big, round eyes.

They looked down at him. Jeff began to ___run___. He

was ___afraid___. A rabbit ran across his ___path___.

Then he heard another ___noise___. It was his ___dog___,

Rags. Jeff was ___glad___ to see ___Rags___!

Name
_____

Critical Thinking, Level B © 1993 Steck-Vaughn

Teacher Note
Read the words in the Word Box to pupils. Then tell them that some of the words are missing in this story and that they should be able to tell from the rest of the sentence which words to use. Allow time for independent work.

If you said that something is either **here** or **gone**, you would be right. But, if you said that people have either brown or blue eyes, you would not be right. Some people have green eyes.

Put an **X** before each sentence that is not right because there may be more than two ways it can be.

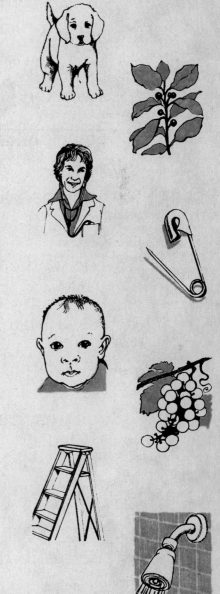

__X__ 1. A dog may be either black or white.

_____ 2. A branch may either have leaves or be bare.

_____ 3. A doctor may be either a man or a woman.

_____ 4. A safety pin may be either open or closed.

_____ 5. A baby may be either a boy or a girl.

__X__ 6. Fruit may be either grapes or oranges.

_____ 7. You may go either up or down on a ladder.

__X__ 8. Water may be either hot or cold.

Name _____

Teacher Note
Go over introductory material with pupils. Emphasize that some either-or statements are correct and some are wrong. Have pupils discuss the sentences they marked with an X. Ask them what some of the other possibilities are that make those sentences false.

Put **X** before each sentence that is probably not all true. Then underline the word that could be changed to make the sentence true.

X _____ 1. Roy's parents let <u>all</u> the kids play in their yard.

X _____ 2. They can <u>always</u> go swimming.

_____ 3. Some children have pets.

_____ 4. Nine people are going on this trip.

X _____ 5. This is the <u>best</u> cereal of all.

X _____ 6. <u>All</u> of Mike's clothes are new, so why can't I have some?

X _____ 7. We're the <u>only</u> ones that don't have a swimming pool.

_____ 8. There will be a big circus in town soon.

X _____ 9. <u>Nobody</u> will be wearing dresses to the party.

X _____ 10. <u>Everybody</u> knows that joke.

Name _____

Teacher Note
Discuss the use of loaded words and slanted arguments. For example, if you tell your Mom that all the children in school have sweatshirts with the school's name on them in order to make her feel she should buy one for you, the word *all* is a loaded word. Have pupils finish the page independently.

A. Judging Completeness

Three people have forgotten to put on a part of their special suits. Draw the missing things where they belong.

B. Thinking About Facts That Fit

Imagine the captain asks you to come on the flight. Write a question you would ask before saying **yes** or **no**.

Answers will vary.

C. Logic of Actions

Suzi will be a reporter on the space trip. When she returns, she will tell her classmates about the trip, and show them pictures. Name two things she should take.

Answers will vary.

Name

Teacher Note
After completing the page, pupils may discuss and check their work with you or a partner.

D. Story Logic
Parts of a Story
Recognizing True and False

Read the poem. Then answer the questions.

Pie Problem

If I eat one more piece of pie, I'll die!
If I can't have one more piece of pie, I'll die!
So since it's all decided I must die,
I might as well have one more piece of pie.
MMMM—OOH—MY!
Chomp—Gulp—'Bye.

Shel Silverstein from A LIGHT IN THE ATTIC

1. Has the speaker eaten any pie yet? _____yes_____

2. Could the speaker really die? _____no_____

3. What happened at the end of the poem?

   _____He ate another piece._____

E. Abstract or Concrete

Write your own poem on a sheet of paper. Tell about something you cannot hold or touch. Use the Idea Box to help you get started.

Idea Box

| friendship |
| love   fear |
| anger |

Name _____

Teacher Note
After completing the page, pupils may discuss and check their work with you or a partner.